THIS BOOK BELONGS TO

The Library of

....

....

Thank you for Purchasing my book and taking the time to read it from front to back. I am always grateful when a reader chooses my work and I hope you enjoyed it!

With the vast selection available online, I am touched that you chose to be purchasing my work and take valuable time out of your life to read it. My hope is that you feel you made the right decision.

I very much would like to know what you thought of the book. Please take the time to write an honest and informative review on Amazon.com. Your experience and opinions will be of great benefit to me and those readers looking to make an informed choice.

With much thanks.

Table of Contents

SUMMARY

The Artistic Appeal of Catherine Wheel and Bavarian Stitches in Crochet: Crochet, a popular craft that involves creating fabric by interlocking loops of yarn or thread using a crochet hook, offers a wide range of techniques and stitches that can be used to create intricate and visually appealing designs. Among these techniques, Catherine Wheel and Bavarian stitches stand out for their artistic appeal and ability to add depth and texture to crochet projects.

The Catherine Wheel stitch, also known as the starburst stitch, is a versatile and eye-catching stitch that creates a circular pattern resembling the spokes of a wheel. This stitch is achieved by working multiple stitches into the same stitch or space, creating a cluster of stitches that radiate outwards. The result is a stunning design that can be used to create various crochet items such as blankets, scarves, and even garments. The Catherine Wheel stitch is particularly popular for its ability to create a sense of movement and dimension in crochet projects, making them visually captivating and unique.

On the other hand, Bavarian stitches, also known as the Bavarian square or the Bavarian crochet, are a more complex and intricate stitch pattern that originated in Bavaria, Germany. This stitch involves working multiple rounds of stitches in different colors, creating a textured and three-dimensional effect. The Bavarian stitch is characterized by its geometric shapes and intricate patterns, making it a favorite among crocheters who enjoy challenging and detailed projects.

What sets the Bavarian stitch apart is its ability to create a raised and embossed effect, giving the crochet fabric a quilted or padded appearance. This stitch is often used to create blankets, pillows, and other home decor items that require a touch of elegance and sophistication. The Bavarian stitch can also be combined with other stitches and techniques to create unique and visually stunning designs, making it a versatile choice for crocheters looking to push their creative boundaries.

Both the Catherine Wheel and Bavarian stitches offer crocheters the opportunity to explore their artistic side and create visually striking and unique crochet projects. These stitches not only add depth and texture to the fabric but also allow for endless possibilities in terms of color combinations and design variations. Whether you are a beginner or an experienced crocheter, incorporating these stitches into your projects can elevate your crochet work to a whole new level.

In conclusion, the artistic appeal of Catherine Wheel and Bavarian stitches in crochet lies in their ability to create visually captivating designs that add depth, texture, and dimension to crochet projects.

Navigating Through This Comprehensive Guide in Crochet: Welcome to this comprehensive guide on navigating through the world of crochet! Whether you are a beginner or an experienced crocheter looking to expand your skills, this guide is designed to provide you with all the information you need to successfully navigate through the various aspects of crochet.

Crochet is a versatile and creative craft that involves using a hook and yarn to create beautiful and intricate designs. From simple stitches to complex patterns, there is something for everyone in the world of crochet. However, with so many different techniques, tools, and resources available, it can sometimes feel overwhelming to know where to start or how to progress in your crochet journey.

That's where this guide comes in. We have carefully curated a collection of information, tips, and tutorials to help you navigate through the different aspects of crochet. Whether you are looking to learn the basics, explore new stitches, or tackle more advanced projects, this guide has got you covered.

To begin, we will start with the basics of crochet. We will cover the essential tools and materials you will need, such as hooks, yarn, and other accessories. We will also explain the different types of yarn and their uses, as well as provide guidance on choosing the right hook size for your project.

Once you have your tools and materials ready, we will dive into the fundamental stitches of crochet. We will explain each stitch in detail, providing step-by-step instructions and accompanying visuals to help you understand and practice each technique. From the basic chain stitch to more complex stitches like the double crochet and treble crochet, you will learn how to create a variety of textures and patterns.

After mastering the basic stitches, we will move on to exploring different crochet techniques. We will introduce you to techniques such as colorwork, lacework, and amigurumi, and provide tutorials and tips to help you incorporate these techniques into your projects. Whether you want to create intricate lace shawls, colorful blankets, or adorable stuffed animals, this guide will equip you with the knowledge and skills to bring your ideas to life.

In addition to the technical aspects of crochet, we will also cover other important topics such as reading crochet patterns, understanding abbreviations and symbols, and troubleshooting common mistakes. We will provide guidance on how to decipher pattern instructions, make modifications to suit your preferences, and fix any errors that may arise during your crochet journey.

Furthermore, this guide will also introduce you to the vibrant and supportive crochet community. We will provide information on online resources, forums, and social media

Crochet Essentials for Beginners: Crochet Essentials for Beginners is a comprehensive guide that covers all the necessary tools, materials, and techniques needed to start your crochet journey. Whether you are a complete novice or have some basic knowledge, this book will provide you with the essential information to get started and progress in your crochet skills.

The book begins by introducing the basic crochet tools that every beginner should have. It explains the different types of crochet hooks, their sizes, and materials, helping you choose the right one for your projects. It also covers other essential tools such as yarn needles, stitch markers, and measuring tape, and explains their importance in the crochet process.

Next, the book dives into the world of yarns. It explains the different types of yarn fibers, their weights, and how to choose the right yarn for your projects. It also provides tips on yarn substitutions and how to read yarn labels, ensuring that you make informed decisions when purchasing yarn.

Once you have your tools and yarn ready, the book moves on to teaching you the basic crochet stitches. It starts with the foundation chain, single crochet, double crochet, and half-double crochet stitches, gradually building your skills and confidence. Each stitch is explained in detail, with step-by-step instructions and clear illustrations, making it easy for beginners to follow along.

As you progress through the book, you will learn more advanced stitches such as treble crochet, shell stitch, and popcorn stitch. The book also covers different crochet techniques, including working in the round, changing colors, and creating texture through various stitch patterns. With each new stitch and technique, the book provides practice exercises and small projects to help you apply what you have learned.

In addition to the technical aspects of crochet, the book also covers important topics such as tension control, gauge swatching, and troubleshooting common mistakes. It emphasizes the importance of practicing and experimenting with different techniques to improve your skills and develop your own crochet style.

To inspire and motivate beginners, the book includes a collection of beginner-friendly crochet patterns. These patterns range from simple scarves and hats to more complex projects like blankets and amigurumi toys. Each pattern is accompanied by detailed instructions, stitch diagrams, and helpful tips, ensuring that you can successfully complete the projects and showcase your newfound crochet skills.

Crochet Essentials for Beginners is not just a guidebook; it is a companion that will support you throughout your crochet journey. With its comprehensive coverage of tools, materials, techniques, and patterns, this book is a valuable resource for anyone who wants

Understanding Crochet: Tools, Materials, and Basic Concepts:

Crochet is a popular craft that involves creating fabric by interlocking loops of yarn or thread using a crochet hook. It is a versatile and creative hobby that allows you to make a wide range of items, from clothing and accessories to home decor and toys. To get started with crochet, it is important to understand the tools, materials, and basic concepts involved.

Tools:

The main tool you will need for crochet is a crochet hook. These hooks come in various sizes, which determine the size of the stitches you create. The size of the hook you choose will depend on the thickness of the yarn or thread you are using and the desired outcome of your project. Additionally, you may also need a pair of scissors, a tape measure, stitch markers, and a yarn needle for finishing touches.

Materials:

The choice of yarn or thread is crucial in crochet, as it determines the look and feel of your finished project. Yarn comes in different weights, ranging from super fine to super bulky, and can be made from various fibers such as cotton, wool, acrylic, or blends. The weight of the yarn you choose will depend on the type of project you are working on. Thinner yarns are ideal for delicate items like lace doilies, while thicker yarns are better suited for cozy blankets or scarves. Similarly, the type of fiber you choose will affect the drape, warmth, and care instructions of your finished piece.

Basic Concepts:

Crochet is based on a few basic stitches that are used to create different patterns and textures. The most common stitches include the chain stitch (ch), single crochet (sc), double crochet (dc), and treble crochet (tr). These stitches are combined in various ways to create different patterns, such as granny squares, ripple stitches, or cables. Learning these basic stitches and understanding how they are worked together will allow you to follow crochet patterns and create your own designs.

In addition to stitches, it is important to understand other concepts in crochet, such as gauge and tension. Gauge refers to the number of stitches and rows per inch in a crochet fabric and is important for ensuring that your finished project matches the measurements specified in a pattern. Tension, on the other hand, refers to how tightly or loosely you hold the yarn and hook while crocheting. Consistent tension is important for creating even stitches and preventing your project from becoming too tight or too loose.

Mastering Fundamental Stitches and Techniques in Crochet: Mastering Fundamental Stitches and Techniques in Crochet is a comprehensive guide that aims to equip beginners and intermediate crocheters with the necessary skills and knowledge to create beautiful and intricate crochet projects. This book is designed to be a valuable resource for anyone interested in learning or improving their crochet skills.

The book begins with an introduction to the basic tools and materials needed for crochet, including different types of yarn, hooks, and other accessories. It also provides a detailed explanation of how to read crochet patterns and charts, ensuring that readers are able to understand and follow instructions accurately.

The next section of the book focuses on teaching the fundamental stitches in crochet. Each stitch is explained in a step-by-step manner, accompanied by clear illustrations and photographs. From the basic chain stitch to more complex stitches like the double crochet and treble crochet, readers will gain a solid foundation in crochet techniques.

Once the fundamental stitches have been mastered, the book progresses to more advanced techniques. Readers will learn how to create different types of crochet fabric, such as textured stitches, lace patterns, and colorwork. The book also covers shaping techniques, including increasing and decreasing stitches, as well as joining techniques for seamless crochet projects.

In addition to teaching stitches and techniques, the book also provides guidance on choosing the right yarn and hook size for different projects. It offers tips and tricks for achieving consistent tension and gauge, ensuring that readers are able to create professional-looking crochet pieces.

To further enhance the learning experience, the book includes a variety of crochet patterns that allow readers to practice and apply the techniques they have learned. These patterns range from simple projects like scarves and hats to more complex items like blankets and garments. Each pattern is accompanied by detailed instructions, stitch diagrams, and full-color photographs, making it easy for readers to follow along and create their own beautiful crochet projects.

Overall, Mastering Fundamental Stitches and Techniques in Crochet is a comprehensive and user-friendly guide that covers everything a beginner or intermediate crocheter needs to know. Whether you are just starting out or looking to expand your crochet skills, this book is sure to be a valuable resource that will inspire and empower you to create stunning crochet pieces.

Deciphering Crochet Patterns and Abbreviations in Crochet: Deciphering crochet patterns and understanding the abbreviations used in crochet can be a daunting task for beginners. However, with a little practice and patience, you can easily decode these patterns and create beautiful crochet projects.

Crochet patterns are written instructions that guide you through the process of creating a specific crochet item. They include information about the stitches, yarn, hook size, and any additional techniques or special instructions required. These patterns are typically written using a combination of abbreviations and symbols, which can be confusing if you're not familiar with them.

To begin deciphering a crochet pattern, it's important to understand the basic crochet stitches. These include the chain stitch (ch), slip stitch (sl st), single crochet (sc), half double crochet (hdc), double crochet (dc), and treble crochet (tr). Familiarizing yourself with these stitches will make it easier to understand the instructions in the pattern.

In addition to the basic stitches, crochet patterns often use abbreviations to represent specific techniques or combinations of stitches. For example, the pattern may instruct you to work a dc2tog which means to work a double crochet decrease by combining two double crochet stitches into one. Other common abbreviations include yo for yarn over, st for stitch, rep for repeat, and inc for increase.

It's important to note that different crochet patterns may use slightly different abbreviations, so it's always a good idea to refer to the pattern's key or glossary for clarification. Additionally, some patterns may include symbols or diagrams to further illustrate the stitches and techniques used.

When reading a crochet pattern, it's helpful to break it down into smaller sections and read through each step carefully. Take note of any special instructions or variations in stitch counts. It can also be helpful to highlight or underline the abbreviations as you go along to keep track of what each one represents.

If you're still having trouble deciphering a crochet pattern, don't be afraid to seek help from more experienced crocheters. Online forums, crochet groups, and tutorial videos can provide valuable guidance and clarification.

Once you've successfully deciphered a crochet pattern, it's time to put your skills to the test and start crocheting! Remember to take your time, practice the stitches, and refer back to the pattern as needed. With practice, you'll become more comfortable with reading and understanding crochet patterns, allowing you to tackle more complex projects with confidence.

Organizing Your Crochet Space and Materials in Crochet: Organizing your crochet space and materials is essential for any crochet enthusiast. Having a well-organized space not only makes it easier to find your supplies but also allows for a more enjoyable and efficient crochet experience.

One of the first steps in organizing your crochet space is to assess the available storage options. Consider the size of your space and the amount of materials you have. Look for storage solutions that maximize the use of vertical space, such as shelves or hanging organizers. Utilizing clear bins or containers can also be helpful, as they allow you to easily see what is inside without having to open each one.

Next, it's important to categorize your materials. Sort your yarn by color, weight, or project type. This will make it easier to find the specific yarn you need for a project and prevent you from buying duplicates. You can use labels or dividers to keep everything organized within your storage containers.

In addition to yarn, you may have other crochet tools and accessories that need to be organized. Consider using small containers or pouches to store your crochet hooks, stitch markers, and scissors. Having designated spaces for each item will save you time and frustration when you need to find them.

Another aspect of organizing your crochet space is creating a comfortable and functional work area. Ensure that you have a comfortable chair and good lighting to prevent strain on your eyes and body. Keep a small table or tray nearby to hold your current project and any necessary tools. This will help keep your work area tidy and prevent any accidental damage to your project.

Lastly, don't forget to regularly declutter and reorganize your crochet space. As you complete projects and acquire new materials, it's important to reassess your storage needs. Take the time to go through your supplies and remove any items that you no longer need or use. This will help keep your space clutter-free and make it easier to find what you need.

In conclusion, organizing your crochet space and materials is a crucial step in creating a productive and enjoyable crochet experience. By utilizing storage solutions, categorizing your materials, and creating a functional work area, you can ensure that your crochet space is efficient and clutter-free. Regularly decluttering and reorganizing will help maintain this organization over time. So, take the time to organize your crochet space and enjoy the benefits of a well-organized and inspiring environment for your crochet projects.

Selecting Suitable Yarns and Colors for Projects in Crochet: When it comes to crochet projects, one of the most important decisions you'll have to make is selecting the suitable yarns and colors. The yarn you choose can greatly impact the final outcome of your project, so it's crucial to consider various factors before making a decision.

Firstly, you need to consider the type of project you're working on. Different projects require different types of yarns. For example, if you're making a blanket, you'll want to choose a yarn that is soft and cozy, such as a bulky or worsted weight yarn. On the other hand, if you're making a delicate lace doily, you'll want to opt for a finer weight yarn, such as lace or fingering weight.

Next, you should consider the fiber content of the yarn. Yarns can be made from a variety of materials, including wool, cotton, acrylic, and blends of different fibers. Each fiber has its own unique characteristics, so it's important to choose one that suits your project. For instance, wool yarns are known for their warmth and elasticity, making them ideal for winter accessories like hats and scarves. Cotton yarns, on the other hand, are breathable and absorbent, making them perfect for summer garments like tank tops and beach cover-ups.

Another factor to consider is the color of the yarn. The color you choose can greatly impact the overall look and feel of your project. If you're making a baby blanket, you might want to choose soft pastel colors to create a soothing and calming effect. On the other hand, if you're making a statement piece like a shawl or a sweater, you might want to opt for bold and vibrant colors to make a bold fashion statement.

It's also important to consider the availability and cost of the yarn. Some yarns may be more readily available in your local craft stores, while others may need to be ordered online. Additionally, certain yarns may be more expensive than others, so it's important to consider your budget when making your selection.

Lastly, it's always a good idea to swatch before starting your project. Swatching involves crocheting a small sample using the chosen yarn and hook size to determine the gauge and ensure that the yarn is suitable for your project. This step can help you avoid any surprises or disappointments once you start working on your actual project.

Tips for a Comfortable and Enjoyable Crochet Experience: Crocheting is a wonderful and relaxing hobby that allows you to create beautiful and unique items. However, in order to have a comfortable and enjoyable crochet experience, there are a few tips and tricks that can greatly enhance your overall experience.

First and foremost, it is important to choose the right crochet hook for your project. Crochet hooks come in various sizes and materials, and selecting the appropriate one can make a significant difference in your comfort level. If you are working with a thicker yarn, opt for a larger hook size, while a smaller hook size is ideal for finer yarns. Additionally, consider the material of the hook - some crocheters prefer the smoothness of metal hooks, while others find comfort in the grip of a wooden or ergonomic hook.

Another crucial aspect of a comfortable crochet experience is maintaining good posture and hand positioning. It is essential to sit in a comfortable chair with proper back support, as this will prevent strain on your back and neck. Additionally, make sure to keep your wrists and hands in a relaxed position, avoiding any unnecessary tension. Taking regular breaks and stretching your hands and fingers can also help prevent fatigue and discomfort.

Furthermore, investing in high-quality yarn can greatly enhance your crochet experience. While it may be tempting to opt for cheaper options, lower-quality yarns can be rough and prone to splitting, making the crocheting process less enjoyable. Choosing soft and smooth yarns will not only feel more comfortable in your hands but also result in a more polished finished product.

In addition to the physical aspects, creating a comfortable and enjoyable crochet environment is equally important. Ensure that you have adequate lighting to avoid straining your eyes, especially when working with darker yarn colors. Organizing your crochet supplies and keeping them within reach will save you time and frustration, allowing you to fully immerse yourself in the crochet process.

Lastly, don't forget to enjoy the journey of crocheting. Embrace the learning process and don't be afraid to try new stitches or patterns. Crocheting should be a relaxing and enjoyable experience, so take the time to savor each stitch and appreciate the progress you make with each project.

In conclusion, by following these tips for a comfortable and enjoyable crochet experience, you can enhance your overall satisfaction and productivity. From selecting the right hook and yarn to maintaining good posture and creating a conducive crochet environment, these small adjustments can make a significant difference in your enjoyment of this wonderful craft.

Origins and Characteristics of Catherine Wheel Stitch in Crochet: The Catherine Wheel stitch is a popular and visually stunning crochet stitch that adds a unique and intricate texture to any project. This stitch is named after the Catherine wheel, a medieval torture device that resembles a spinning wheel with spikes. While the name may sound intimidating, the Catherine Wheel stitch is anything but torturous to create.

The origins of the Catherine Wheel stitch can be traced back to traditional Irish crochet, which is known for its intricate and delicate designs. This stitch was often used to create decorative motifs and lace patterns in Irish crochet garments and accessories. Over time, the Catherine Wheel stitch gained popularity and spread to other crochet traditions around the world.

The Catherine Wheel stitch is characterized by its circular pattern, which resembles the spokes of a wheel. It is created by working multiple stitches into the same stitch or chain space, which creates a cluster of stitches that radiate outwards. This cluster is then surrounded by chains or single crochet stitches, which further enhance the wheel-like appearance of the stitch.

To create the Catherine Wheel stitch, crocheters typically start with a foundation chain and then work a row of double crochet stitches. The next row is where the magic happens, as crocheters begin to create the wheel-like pattern. This is achieved by working a set number of stitches into the same stitch or chain space, followed by chains or single crochet stitches to separate each cluster. The process is repeated across the row, resulting in a visually striking pattern that resembles a spinning wheel.

One of the reasons why the Catherine Wheel stitch is so beloved by crocheters is its versatility. This stitch can be used to create a wide range of projects, from blankets and scarves to hats and shawls. The intricate texture of the Catherine Wheel stitch adds depth and visual interest to any design, making it a popular choice for those looking to create eye-catching and unique crochet pieces.

While the Catherine Wheel stitch may appear complex, it is actually quite simple to learn and master with a bit of practice. There are numerous tutorials and patterns available online that provide step-by-step instructions on how to create this stitch. With a little patience and creativity, crocheters of all skill levels can incorporate the Catherine Wheel stitch into their projects and enjoy the beauty and elegance it brings to their crochet work.

Basic Instructions and Practice Swatch for Catherine Wheel Stitch in Crochet: The Catherine Wheel stitch is a beautiful and intricate crochet stitch that creates a stunning circular pattern. If you're new to this stitch or just need a refresher, this guide will provide you with basic instructions and a practice swatch to help you master the Catherine Wheel stitch.

To begin, you'll need a crochet hook and yarn of your choice. It's recommended to use a medium weight yarn and a corresponding hook size to ensure that your stitches are even and well-defined.

Step 1: Foundation Chain

Start by creating a foundation chain of any desired length. The length of your chain will determine the width of your swatch or project. Make sure to chain an even number of stitches to maintain the symmetry of the Catherine Wheel stitch.

Step 2: First Row

Once you have your foundation chain, skip the first three chains and double crochet into the fourth chain from the hook. Double crochet into each chain across the row. This will create a row of double crochet stitches.

Step 3: Second Row

To begin the second row, chain three and turn your work. This chain three will count as the first double crochet stitch of the row. Double crochet into the next stitch, and then create a Catherine Wheel stitch in the following stitch.

To create a Catherine Wheel stitch, yarn over and insert your hook into the next stitch. Pull up a loop, yarn over again, and pull through two loops on your hook. Repeat this process four more times, creating a total of six loops on your hook. Yarn over once more and pull through all six loops to complete the Catherine Wheel stitch.

Continue alternating between a regular double crochet stitch and a Catherine Wheel stitch across the row. End the row with a double crochet stitch in the last stitch.

Step 4: Repeat Rows

To create the Catherine Wheel stitch pattern, repeat the second row for as many rows as desired. Each row will consist of alternating regular double crochet stitches and Catherine Wheel stitches.

Step 5: Finishing

Once you've completed your desired number of rows, finish off your work by cutting the yarn and pulling it through the last loop on your hook. Weave in any loose ends to secure them and give your swatch a polished look.

Now that you have the basic instructions for the Catherine Wheel stitch, it's time to practice! Use the instructions above to create a small swatch of the stitch. This will allow you to familiarize yourself with the stitch pattern and perfect your tension and technique.

Understanding Color Changes and Variations in Crochet:

A Comprehensive Guide

Introduction:

Crochet is a versatile and creative craft that allows individuals to create beautiful and intricate designs using yarn and a crochet hook. One of the key elements that can greatly enhance the visual appeal of crochet projects is the use of color. Understanding how to effectively incorporate color changes and variations can elevate your crochet work to a whole new level. In this guide, we will delve into the intricacies of color changes in crochet, exploring different techniques, tips, and tricks to help you master this aspect of the craft.

Section 1: Basics of Color Changes

1.1 Choosing the Right Yarn:

The first step in understanding color changes in crochet is selecting the right yarn. Different yarns have varying color palettes, and it is important to consider factors such as fiber content, weight, and dye lots when making your selection. We will discuss how these factors can impact color changes and provide guidance on making informed choices.

1.2 Understanding Color Theory:

To effectively incorporate color changes in crochet, it is essential to have a basic understanding of color theory. We will explore concepts such as color harmony, complementary colors, and color schemes, and how they can be applied to create visually appealing crochet projects. Additionally, we will discuss the psychological impact of colors and how they can evoke different emotions and moods.

Section 2: Techniques for Color Changes

2.1 Changing Colors in Rows:

One of the most common techniques for color changes in crochet is changing colors in rows. We will provide step-by-step instructions on how to seamlessly transition from one color to another, ensuring clean and professional-looking results. We will also cover techniques for carrying yarn along the edges to minimize loose ends and achieve a neat finish.

2.2 Changing Colors in Rounds:

Crocheting in rounds presents a unique set of challenges when it comes to color changes. We will explore different methods for changing colors in rounds, including the invisible join technique and the jogless join technique. These techniques will enable you to create seamless color transitions in projects such as hats, amigurumi, and mandalas.

2.3 Introducing Variegated Yarn:

Variegated yarn, with its multiple colors and color changes within a single skein, can add depth and complexity to crochet projects. We will discuss techniques for working with variegated yarn, including strategies for managing color pooling and creating intentional color patterns.

Basic Principles of Crochet Design: The basic principles of crochet design encompass a wide range of techniques and concepts that are essential for creating beautiful and functional crochet projects. These principles include understanding the different types of stitches, color theory, pattern design, and project planning.

One of the fundamental aspects of crochet design is having a solid understanding of the various types of stitches. Crochet stitches can range from simple and basic, such as the single crochet and double crochet, to more complex and intricate stitches like the shell stitch or the popcorn stitch. Each stitch has its own unique characteristics and can be used to create different textures and patterns in a crochet project. By mastering these stitches, a crocheter can have more creative freedom and flexibility in their designs.

Color theory is another important principle in crochet design. Understanding how colors interact with each other can greatly enhance the visual appeal of a crochet project. Color theory involves concepts such as color harmony, contrast, and balance. By choosing the right color combinations, a crocheter can create a project that is visually pleasing and harmonious. Additionally, color can be used to highlight certain aspects of a design or to create a specific mood or atmosphere.

Pattern design is a crucial aspect of crochet design. A pattern is essentially a set of instructions that guide a crocheter in creating a specific project. Designing a pattern involves determining the stitch pattern, the size and shape of the project, and any additional embellishments or details. A well-designed pattern should be clear, concise, and easy to follow, allowing crocheters of all skill levels to successfully complete the project. Additionally, pattern design also involves considering the overall aesthetic of the project and ensuring that it aligns with the crocheter's vision.

Project planning is the final principle of crochet design. Before starting a crochet project, it is important to plan and prepare accordingly. This involves selecting the appropriate yarn and hook size for the project, estimating the amount of yarn needed, and creating a timeline for completion. Project planning also includes considering the intended use of the project and any specific requirements or preferences of the recipient. By carefully planning and organizing the project, a crocheter can ensure a smooth and successful crochet experience.

In conclusion, the basic principles of crochet design encompass a range of techniques and concepts that are essential for creating beautiful and functional crochet projects. By understanding the different types of stitches, color theory, pattern design, and project planning, a crocheter can enhance their skills and create stunning crochet designs. Whether it's a simple scarf or

Chapter One – Yarn and Hook Basics

Before we cover the stitches and techniques you need to know to crochet, I thought it would be a good idea to go over some basic knowledge about yarn and crochet hooks.

Yarn and Hooks

Yarn comes in three main fibers; animal, plant, and synthetic. Animal fibers include wool, alpaca, cashmere, angora, and silk. Plant fibers used in yarn manufacturing include cotton, soy, hemp, and linen. Synthetic yarns include acrylic, polyester, microfiber, and metallic fibers.

Yarn also comes in seven weights ranging from very fine yarn used for lace, and jumbo yarn used for rugs and large projects. Most yarn falls into the medium, or worsted, weight range of 4. Red Heart Super Saver, Caron Soft, and Lion Brand Heartland area examples of a medium weight yarn suitable for many projects.

	Yarn Weight Chart			
	Weight	Description	Recommended Hook	Stitches in 4"
0	Lace	Fingerling, Size 10 Crochet Thread	Steel 1.6-1.4mm/B-1	32-48
1	Superfine	Sock, Fingerling	2.25-3mm/B-1 to E-4	21-32
2	Fine	Sport, Baby	3.4-4.5mm/E-4 to 7	16-20
3	Light	DK, Light Worsted	4.5-5.5mm/7 to I/9	12-17
4	Medium	Worsted, Afghan, Aran	5.5-6.5mm/I-9 to K-10 ½	11-14
5	Bulky	Chunky, Craft, Rug	6.5-9mm/K-10 ½ to M-13	8-11
6	Super Bulky	Super Bulky, Roving	9-15mm/m-13 to Q	7-9
7	Jumbo	Jumbo, Roving	15mm and up	6 or less

As you can see by this table each weight has a recommended hook size. This hook size will give you a specific gauge. Gauge refers to the number of stitches across four inches of crocheted fabric, and how many rows it take to make up four inches. This information is important to know when you are working a pattern.

Look at the gauge on the pattern, crochet up a small swatch, and compare it to the pattern's gauge. If your swatch is larger, go down a hook size. If your swatch is smaller, go up a hook size.

Crochet hooks come in many different sizes from very fine almost needle point to large plastic jumbo hooks. Most hooks sold in the US have a number designation, but you may find hooks with only a millimeter designation. Here is a handy table to help you choose the correct hook size.

US Size	Millimeter Size

B/1	2.25mm
C/2	2.75mm
D/3	3.25mm
E/4	3.5mm
F/5	3.75mm
G/6	4mm
7	4.5mm
H/8	5mm
I/9	5.5mm
J/10	6mm
K/10 ½	6.5mm
L/11	8mm
M-N/13	9mm
N-P/15	10mm
P/Q	15mm
Q	16mm
S	19mm

How to Hold a Crochet Hook

There are two main ways to hold your hook; pencil and knife. Both are correct so use whichever one feels most comfortable to you.

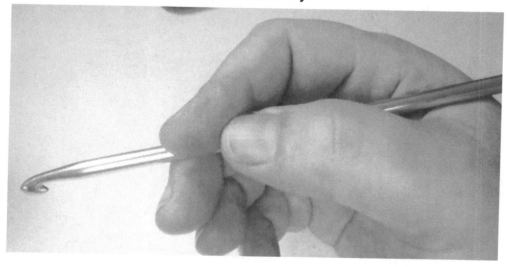

Pencil hold

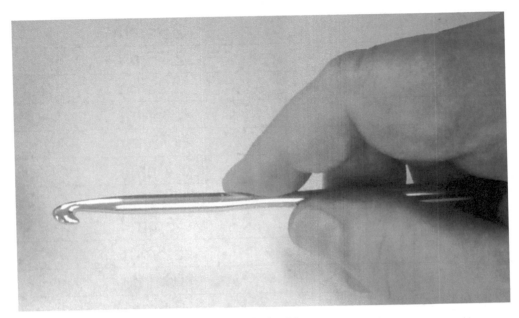

Knife hold

Chapter Two – Basic Crochet Stitches and Techniques

You may already know how to crochet, but in case you don't this chapter will be a complete tutorial on the basic crochet stitches and techniques you need to crochet the stitch patterns in this book. Don't worry if you're a beginner, you can still learn how to crochet the Catherine Wheel and Bavarian Stitch.

Abbreviations

Designers use a standardized set of abbreviations for stitches and instructions. Each pattern should have a key for the abbreviations used in the pattern. Be sure to check it just in case the designer has included unique ones in their pattern. Here are the most common abbreviations used in patterns written in US terms.

Stitch Name	Abbreviation
Chain stitch	Ch
Stitch/Stitches	St/sts
Slip stitch	Sl st
Single crochet	Sc
Double crochet	Dc
Half double crochet	Hdc
Treble crochet	Trb
Repeat	Rep
Single crochet 2 together	Sc2tog
Double crochet 2 together	Dc2tog
Half double crochet 2 together	Hdc2tog

You may also find patterns written in UK terms. Use this table to help translate the abbreviations into US terms.

US Terms		UK Terms	
Chain	Ch	Chain	Ch
Slip stitch	Sl st	Slip stitch	Ss
Single crochet	Sc	Double crochet	Dc
Half double crochet	Hdc	Half treble	Htr
Double crochet	Dc	Treble	Tr
Treble crochet	Trb	Double treble	dtr

Basic Crochet Stitches and Techniques

While you are first learning to crochet, concentrate on handling the hook and yarn. Get used to using them and focus on technique. Take your time and don't worry if you have to rip out (also known as frog) your stitches. We all have to do that sometimes, no matter how proficient we are at crochet. Relax and have fun, remember crochet is supposed to be enjoyable.

Chain Stitch

The chain stitch is used for foundation chains and to create spaces in patterns. First create a slip knot and place it on the hook. Place the yarn over the hook (known as a yarn over) and pull the yarn through the slip knot on the hook. This if the first chain stitch. Yarn over and pull the yarn through the loop on the hook. This is the second chain stitch. Continue this until you have the appropriate number of chain stitches. Concentrate on getting your stitches even and getting used to handling the hook and yarn. Speed will come later, right now concentrate on technique.

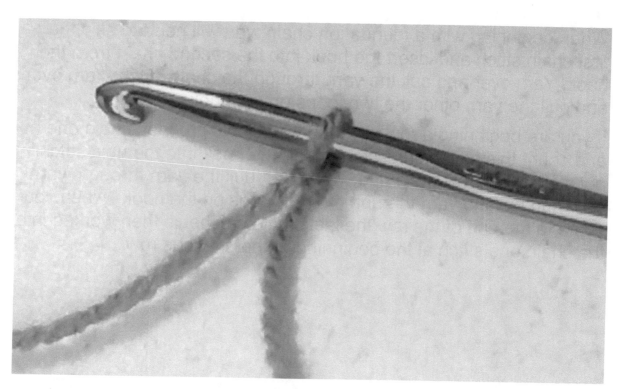

Slip knot

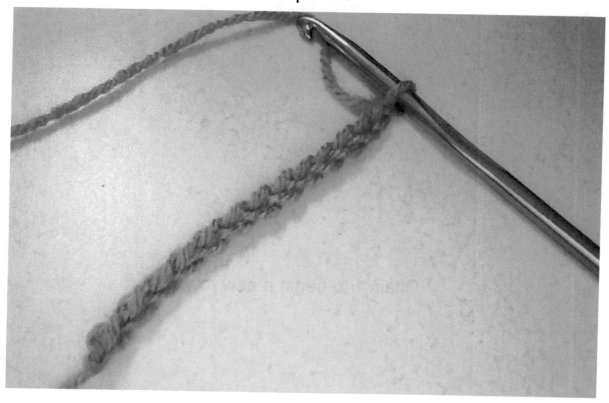

Chain stitch

Single Crochet

When beginning with a foundation chain, you will need to skip the first chain stitch and insert the hook into the second chain from the hook. Yarn over and pull the yarn through the chain stitch. Yarn over and pull the yarn other the two loops on the hook.

If you are beginning a row or round with single crochet, chain one and count this as the first stitch. Insert the hook into the next stitch, not the base of the chain one, yarn over, pull the yarn through, yarn over and pull the yarn through the two loops on the hook. When you come to the end of the row the last single crochet is then worked into the chain one stitch at the beginning of the previous row.

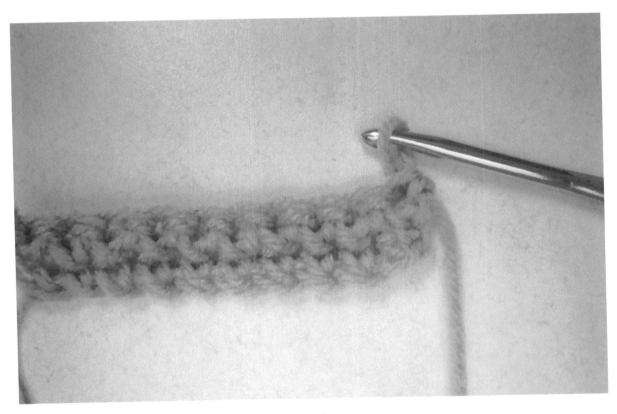

Chain 1 to begin a new row

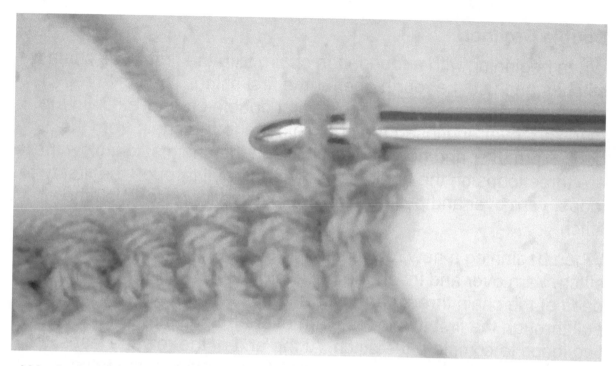

Work the first stitch into the next stitch, not the base of the chain 1.

The last stitch is worked into the chain 1 of the previous row.

Double Crochet

When beginning with a foundation chain, skip the first three chain stitches and use the fourth one for the first stitch. The first three skipped chains are counted as the first double crochet stitch in the row. Yarn over and insert the hook into the fourth chain from the hook. Yarn over and pull the yarn through the chain stitch. Now there are three loops on the hook. Yarn over and pull through the first two loops, yarn over and pull through the last two loops to finish the stitch.

When beginning a new row, chain three. This counts as the first stitch. Yarn over and insert the hook into the next stitch, not into the base of the chain three, yarn over and pull through, yarn over and pull through the first two loops, yarn over and pull through the last two loops to complete the stitch. At the end of the row the last stitch is worked into the third starting chain of the previous row (also known as the turning chain),

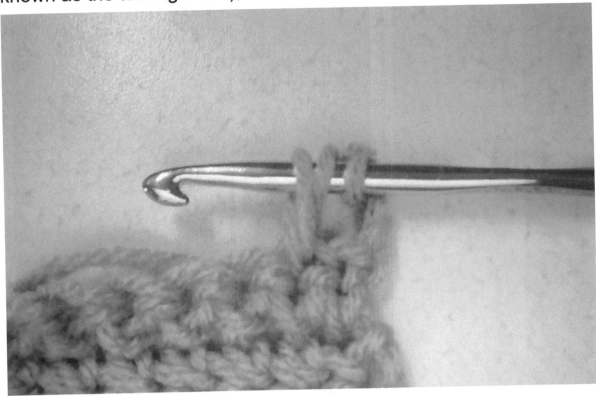

Yarn over and insert the hook into the next stitch, yarn over and pull through.

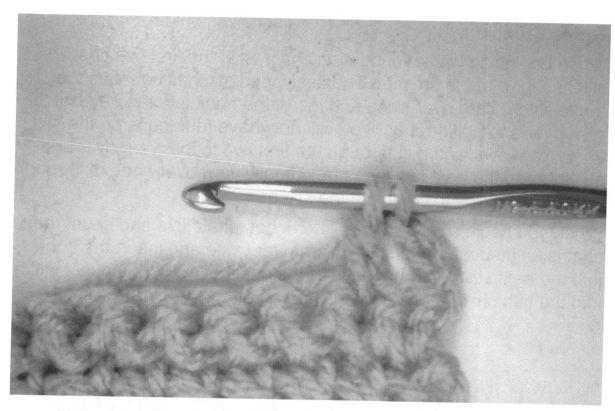

Yarn over and pull through the first two loops on the hook.

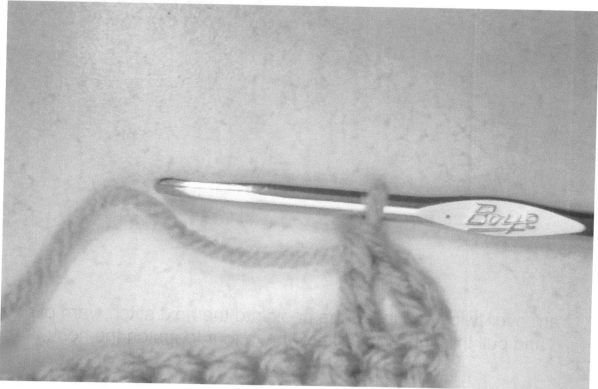

Yarn over and pull through the last two loops to complete the stitch.

Treble Crochet

When beginning with a foundation chain, skip the first five chain stitches for a treble crochet. These skipped stitches count as the first treble stitch. Yarn over twice and insert the hook into the next stitch, yarn over and pull through. You will now have four loops on the hook. Yarn over and pull through the first two loops, yarn over and pull through the next two loops, and finally yarn over and pull through the last two loops to complete the stitch.

When you begin a row with treble crochet, chain five and count these chains as the first treble stitch. Yarn over twice and insert the hook into the next stitch, not the base of the chain five. Work the last stitch into the fifth chain of the turning chain of the previous row.

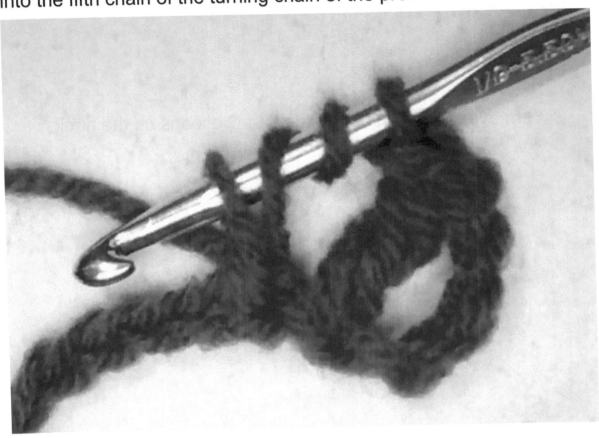

Yarn over twice and insert the hook into the next stitch, yarn over and pull through. You will now have four loops on the hook.

Yarn over and pull through two loops on the hook three times to complete the stitch.

Slip Stitch

A slip stitch is used to join rounds with crocheting in the round, and to move the yarn into the proper place for the next stitch. Insert the hook into the stitch, yarn over and pull the yarn through the stitch and the hook. No stitch is crocheted, but the yarn is moved, or the round is closed.

Front and Back Post Stitches

Each crochet stitch has a post and top loops which form a V shape. Front and back post stitches are worked around the post as opposed to into the top loops of the stitch. These types of stitches are used to create horizontal and vertical ridges in crochet depending on which side of the fabric they are worked. They can also be used to create attractive cables.

On the right side front post stitches create vertical ridges, and on the wrong side they create horizontal ridges. Back post stitches create horizontal ridges on the right side and vertical ridges on the wrong side.

For example, to begin a front post double crochet yarn over and insert the needle from the front to the back around the post of the stitch in the previous row. Yarn over and pull the yarn up even with the stitches in the active row. Yarn over and pull through two loops, yarn over and pull through the last two loops.

The hook goes around the post from front to back.

To crochet a back post double crochet, yarn over and insert the hook from the back to the front around the post. Yarn over and pull the yarn up even with the active stitches, yarn over and pull through two loops, and yarn over and pull through the last two loops to complete the stitch.

The hook goes around the post from back to front. It helps to pinch the fabric a bit to make it easier to insert the hook.

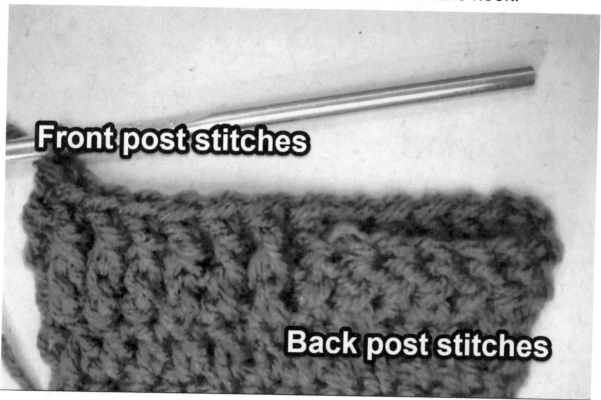

Front post stitches

Back post stitches

Decreases

A decrease is done by crocheting more than one stitch together. For example, if you see the abbreviation dc2tog this mean you will double crochet two stitches as one. Yarn over and insert the hook into the next stitch, yarn over and pull through. Yarn over and pull through the first two loops on the hook. You will have two loops on the hook.

Yarn over and insert the hook into the next stitch, yarn over and pull through. Yarn over and pull through the first two loops on the hook. You now have three loops on the hook. Yarn over and pull the yarn through all three loops at once. This crochets two stitches as one and decreases the number of stitches in a row or round by one.

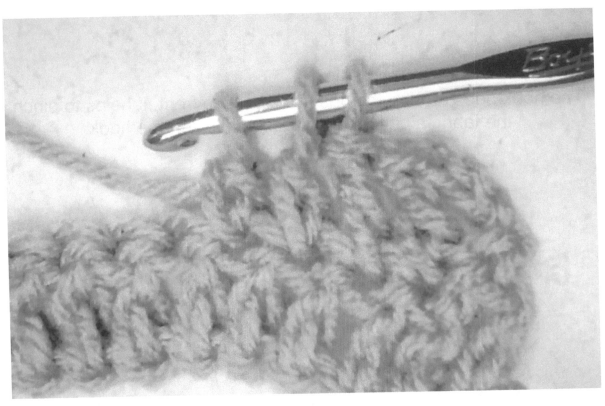

3 loops on the hook

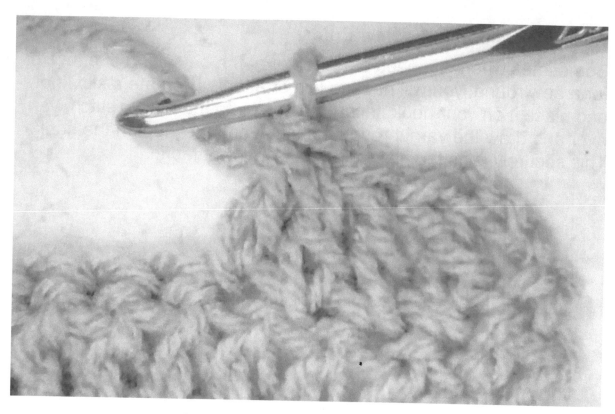

Completed decrease (dc2tog)

Shell Stitches

Shell stitches are created by crocheting more than one stitch into a single stitch. In this example you can see there are three double crochet all worked into one stitch forming a shell.

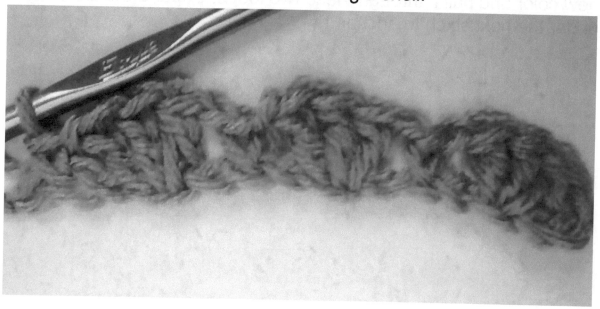

Attaching or Joining a New Color

Sometimes when you need a new color at the beginning of a row, or for a new round, you will need to join or attach it. Create a slip knot and place it on your hook. Insert the hook into the proper stitch, yarn over and draw the yarn through the stitch and the loop on the hook. This securely joins the new color to the crochet fabric.

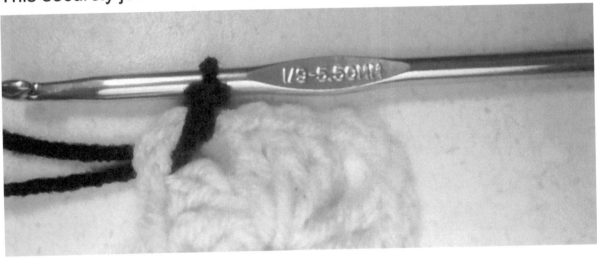

Changing Colors

There will be times when you want to change colors at the beginning of a row, or in a row or round. This is very easy to do. Work the last stitch of the old color until you have two loops on the hook. Grab the new color and pull it through these two loops. Capture the old color under the next stitch to anchor it.

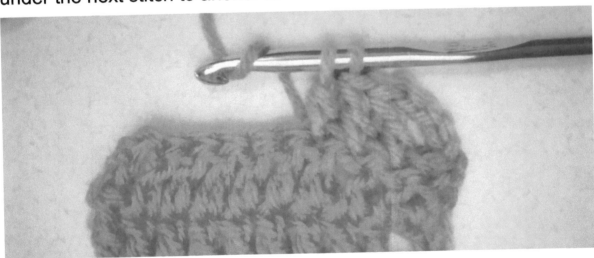

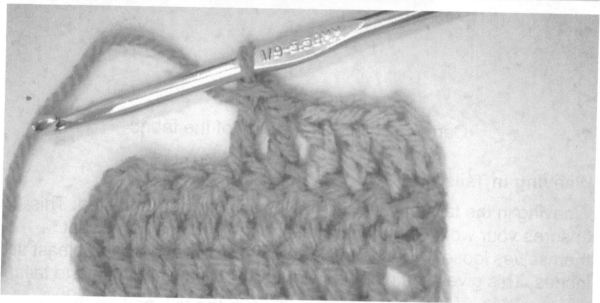

Completed color change

When you are beginning a new row with a new color work the last stitch of the row until you have two loops on the hook and then pull the new color through the loops. Carry the unused color up the side of the fabric by capturing it under the first chain stitch of the next row. This is a handy technique if you plan on alternating colors and don't want to have a ton of tails to weave in. It also makes a very secure and stable fabric.

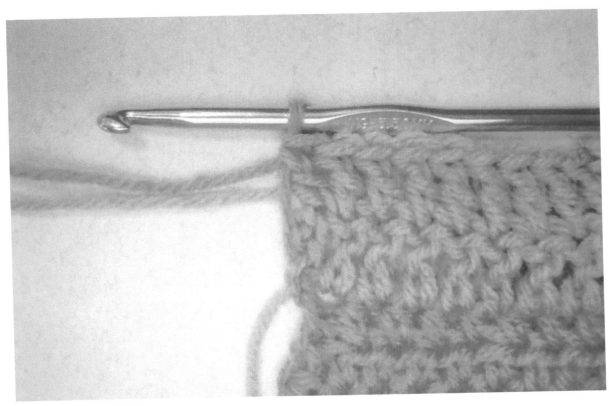

Carrying colors up the side of the fabric

Weaving in Tails

Weaving in the tails of yarn securely is a very important step. This ensures your work doesn't unravel and the stitches don't work themselves loose. When you fasten off yarn always leave at least six inches. This gives you plenty to work with when weaving in the tails.

Thread a blunt end or tapestry needle with the tail, and on the wrong side of the fabric weave the tail in and out of the stitches for about an inch. Turn the fabric and weave the tail in and out of the stitches on the wrong side again for about an inch. Now turn the fabric one last time and weave the tail in and out of the stitches for another inch.

Always turn the fabric at least three times and weave the tails carefully into the stitches on the wrong side of the fabric to secure them. Now you can trim the tail and know that your yarn is secure.

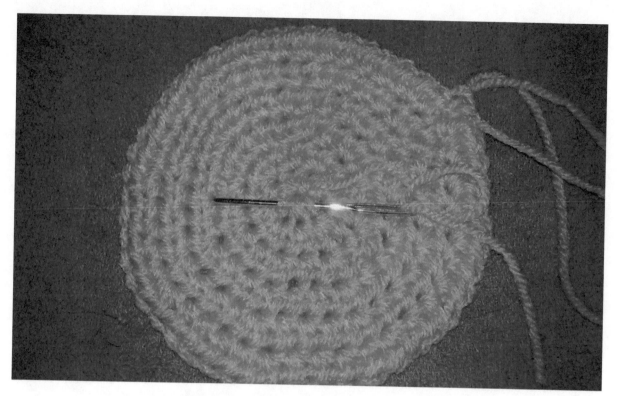

First one way for about an inch

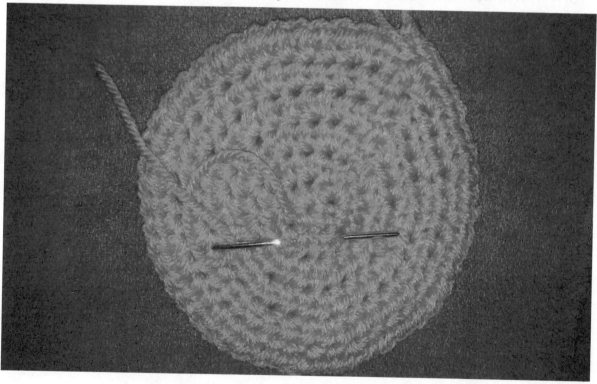

Turn the fabric and weave in for another inch

Turn it one last time and weave in the tail for another inch, now you can cut your yarn and the tail will be secure.

Chapter Three – Catherine Wheel Stitch

The Catherine Wheel Stitch is a very fun pattern to learn. You can use two colors, or use as many colors as you like for a very bright and vibrant look.

When you look at the finished pattern you see that there are circles in the pattern. These circles are actually two parts of the pattern. The bottom circle is crocheted by crocheting seven stitches together and the top of the circle is formed by crocheting seven stitches into the eye of the bottom cluster of seven stitches.

When you crochet a cluster stitch the finishing chain 1 forms the eye. It is into this eye that you will be crocheting the multiple stitches to form the top of the circle.

Crochet the 7 stitch cluster stitch by yarning over and inserting the hook into the next stitch, yarn over and pull through, yarn over and pull through the first 2 loops on the hook. Yarn over and insert the hook into the next stitch, yarn over and pull through, yarn over and pull through the first two loops on the hook. Repeat this five more times. You will have 8 loops on the hook. Yarn over and pull through all 8 loops at once and chain 1 to lock the stitch.

First you need to begin with a foundation chain in sets of 8 plus 2. This means crochet any number of chain stitches that are divisible by 8 and then add 2 more stitches at the end. The first row is the set up row.

Row 1: sc into the 2nd ch from the hook * sk2 chs, 7dc into the next ch st, sk 2 chs, sc into each of the next 3 sts* rep across row ending with a sc into each of the last 2 sts.

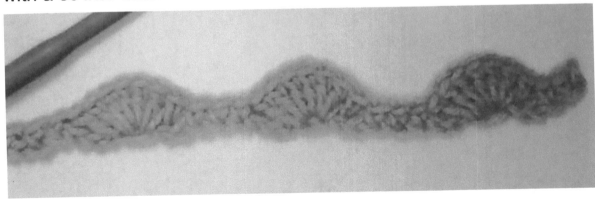

Row 2: Fasten on new color and ch3, dc3tog, ch3, sc into each of the next 3 sts *ch2, dc7tog, ch3, sc into each of the next 3 sts* rep across row to last 4 sts, ch2, dc4tog, ch1, turn

Row 3: ch3, 3dc into the base of the ch3, sc into each of the next 3 sts *7dc into the eye of the dc7tog, sc into each of the next 3 sts* rep across row end with 4dc into the eye of the beginning dc3tog of the previous row, fasten off color

You can see how the dc7tog forms the bottom of the circles and the 7dc into the eye forms the top of the circles.

Row 4: Fasten on new color and ch1 into the same st, sc into the next st *ch2, dc7tog, ch3, sc into each of the next 3 sts* rep across row ending with a sc into the last 2 sts, turn

Row 5: ch1, sc into the base of the ch1, and into the next st *7dc into the eye of the next dc7tog cluster, sc into each of the next 3 sts* rep across row ending with a sc into each of the last 2 sts, turn

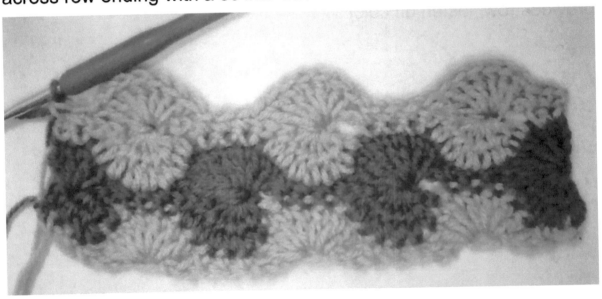

Repeat Rows 2-5 until you have the desired length. To end the project repeat Row 2.

Catherine Wave Stitch

The Catherine Wave Stitch is a variation of the Catherine Wheel stitch. Instead of the halves of the circles being stacked, they are offset which forms a pretty wave pattern. This is a fun and easy variation on the ripple stitch.

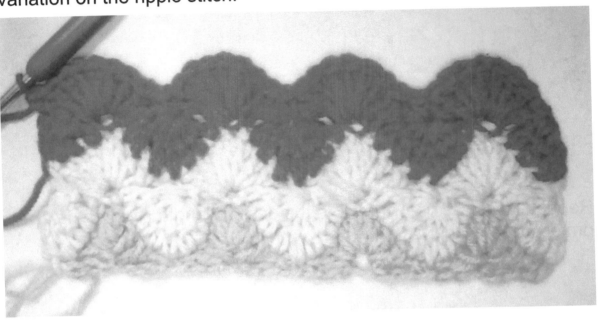

To begin chain a foundation chain in sets of 6 plus 2. When you crochet the first row you will be using the back hump, or spine, of the foundation chain. Turn the chain and look for the little humps on the back and use these for the first row of stitches.

Row 1: sc into the 2nd ch from the hook *sk 2 sts, 7dc into the next st, sk 2 ch, sc into the next ch st* rep across row, fasten off color

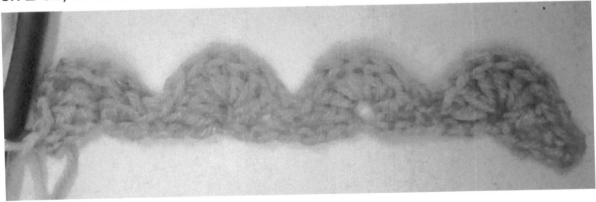

Row 2: Attach new color into last sc, ch3, dc3tog, ch3, sc into next st
ch2, dc7tog, ch2, sc into next st rep across row ending with dc4tog
(remember to ch1 to lock the stitch) turn

Row 3: ch1, sc into the eye of the dc4tog *dc 7 into next sc, sc into
the eye of the next dc7tog cluster* rep across row ending with a sc
into the eye of the dc3tog cluster at the beginning of the previous
row, fasten off color

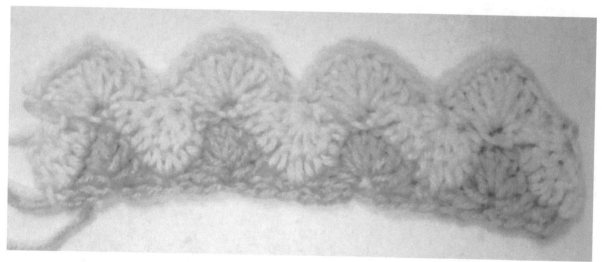

Repeat Rows 2 and 3 to desired length, ending with Row 2 for a
straight edge.

Catherine Wheel Square

You can also use the Catherine Wheel pattern in the round. The end result looks very similar to Bavarian crochet.

Just like in the Catherine Wheel stitch done in rows, the Catherine Wheel crocheted in rounds the circles are crocheted in two parts, the bottom and then the top using cluster and shell stitches.

To begin chain 4 and join with a slip stitch in the first chain to form a ring

Round 1: *sc into the rind, ch4, 4dc cluster st (dc4tog) into the ring, ch5* rep 3 times, join with a sl st into the 1st sc

Round 1

Round 2: ch2, sc into the same st *12dc into the eye of the dc4tog cluster, sc into next sc* rep 3 more times into the eye of each cluster join with a sl st into the beginning sc, fasten off color

Top of circle is formed by 3 sets of 4dc separated by ch2.

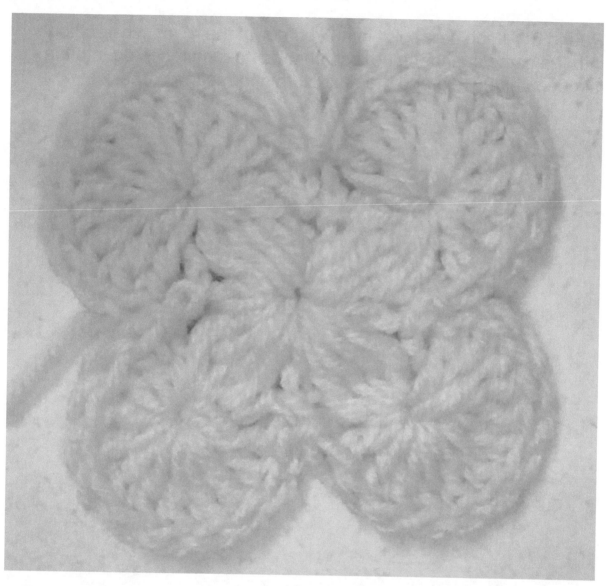

Round 2

Round 3: Attach new color in any corner at the 4th dc, ch1 sc2tog into the same st and the next st, ch4, dc4tog, ch4, sc2tog into the last st of the dc4tog and the next st (this forms the corner)

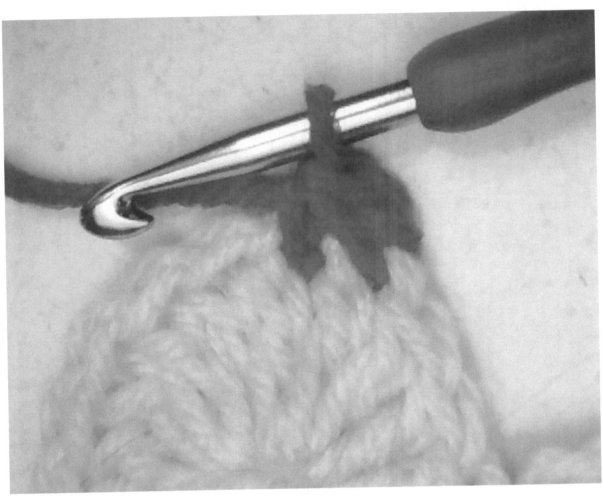

Attach the new color, chain 1 and work sc2tog using the same space as the chain 1 and the next stitch.

The corners are formed by the dc4tog. Use the last dc space and the next stitch for the next sc2tog. Now you need to fill in the sides.

Ch4, sc8tog skipping the middle sc, ch4, sc2tog using the last dc and the next st

Continue around the square using the first stitch as the last stitch for the last cluster, chain 4 and slip stitch into the first sc.

Round 3

Round 4: ch1, sc into the joining slip st, 12 dc into the eye of the corner cluster, sc into the next sc (this forms the top of the corner circle) work 8 dc into the eye of the next cluster, sc into the next sc (this forms the top of the side circle), Continue around the square in this manner, join with a slip stitch into the beginning sc

Work 12dc into the eye of the corner clusters, and 8dc into the side clusters

Continue with this pattern until you reach the desired size.

Chapter Four – Bavarian Stitch

The Bavarian stitch creates a very pretty pattern. It is similar to the Catherine Wheel stitch in that the circles are crocheted in two parts. If you remember to look at each circle as having an upper and lower section, it will make it easier for you to visualize the pattern. You can use different colors or use a long strand variegated yarn to create color changes.

Begin with chain 5. Slip stitch into the first chain to form a ring.

Round 1: *sc into the ring, ch5, 4trbtog into the ring, ch5* rep 3 more times and join with a sl st into the beginning sc (this forms the bottom of the first round of circles)

Close up of corner in Round 2

Round 2: ch1, sc into the joining st *ch2 (4 trb into the center of the eye of the cluster, ch1) rep ( ) 2 more times* rep entire repeat 3 times around and join with a sl st in the beginning sc, fasten off color

Round 2

Round 3: At each new color change you will fasten the new color in the same spot on the corner. Fasten new color into ch1 sp between the first 2 sets of trb shells.

Ch1, sc into the same ch1 sp, ch5, 4bptrtog (4 back post treble crochet together) using the posts of the next 4 sts, ch5, sc into the next ch1 sp

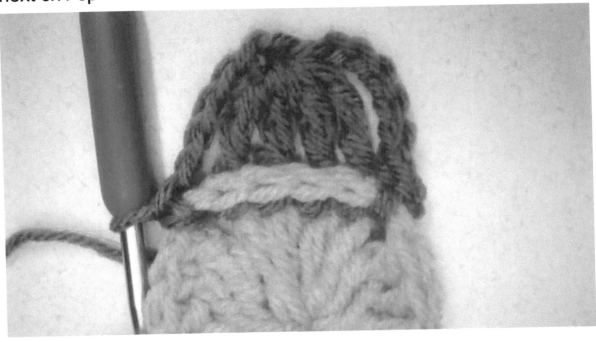

This forms the corner

ch5, bptrb8tog (back post treble crochet 8 together) ignoring the sc in the middle rep the corner and side patterns around the square ending with a sl st into the beginning sc

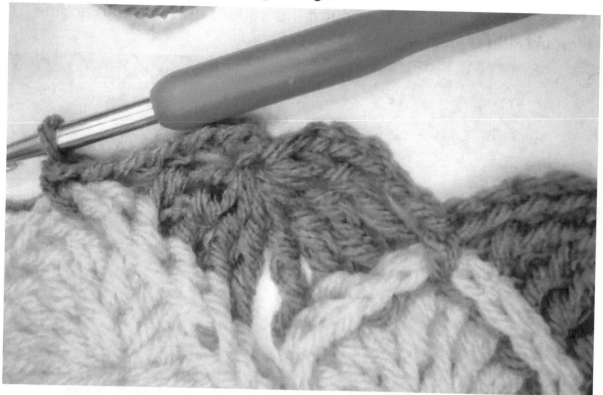

Skip the sc in the middle of the side space

Round 4: ch1, sc into the joining st, 4 trb into the eye of the corner cluster, ch2, 4trb, ch2, 4trb, sc into sc (this completes a corner), into the center of the side 8 bptr cluster work 4trb, ch2, 4trb, sc into the next sc, repeat this pattern around the square and join with a slip stitch into the beginning sc, fasten off color

Round 4

Repeat Rounds 3 and 4 until you have the desires size. The only difference is as your square grows you will have more side sections to crochet. Join the new color in the same space in the corner, between the first and second 4 double crochet clusters each time you fasten on a new color.

Each corner will have 4 back post treble crochet clusters topped by three sections of 4 double crochet shells and chain 1 spaces. Each side section will have 8 back post treble crochet clusters topped by a 4 double crochet shell and two chain 5 sections.

An easy way to think about the pattern is that each circle will have 16 treble crochet in total. So on the corners you have a 4 treble cluster so you need 12 more treble crochet to complete the circle. On the sides each cluster has 8 treble crochet, so you need 8 treble crochet to finish the circle.

By using back post stitches you form a pretty raised ridge between the rounds.

Thank You!

Thank you for purchasing this book on learning the basics of crochet and the Catherine Wheel and Bavarian stitches. I hope you enjoyed learning with me and working up these fun and attractive stitch patterns. Be sure to check out the many videos and online tutorials for these stitches, as well as the many free patterns using these stitches which are available. Until next time, take care and keep on hooking!

KNIT AND PURL TEXTURE IN KNITTING

A Beginners Guide to Texture with Knit and Purl Stitches

By Violet Henderson

Contents

Chapter One – Yarn and Needles

In this chapter we'll learn the basics of yarn and needles. This information is important to learn because you can then choose the correct yarn and needle type for every project.

Yarn

Yarn comes in three main types of fibers; animal, plant, and synthetic. Animal fibers include wool, alpaca, cashmere, angora, and silk. Plant fibers include cotton, hemp, soy, bamboo, and linen. Synthetic fibers include acrylic, polyester, microfiber, and metallic threads. Each type of yarn has its benefits. For example, wool yarn works up into a nice warm spongy fabric, while cotton yarn is stiffer and soaks up moisture. Acrylic yarn is suitable for many projects, and is a cost effective and easy to work with choice for beginners and more advanced knitting artists alike.

Blocking

Animal and plant fiber based yarn looks best if the projects are blocked once you have completed them. Blocking relaxes the yarn fibers and brings out the stitch definition. Blocking is also important for garments so you get the correct fit.

Once you have finished your project soak it in water and then roll it up in a big fluffy towel to remove the excess moisture. Do not ring the towel as this may damage the knitting. On either blocking mats or another big towel take some blocking or sewing pins and begin shaping the project. Pin the outer edges shaping the fabric as needed. You may need to move the pins as you block. Once you're happy with the shape of the fabric, let it dry completely before you take the pins out.

You can also use a spray bottle of water for smaller projects. Pin the fabric onto blocking mats or a big towel and then gently mist the fabric with water. Let dry completely and remove the pins.

While acrylic or synthetic yarn rarely needs to be blocked, you can block them with steam. Pin the fabric onto blocking mats or a big towel and then very carefully use a steam iron and apply steam gently to the fabric. Hold the iron up off the fabric and do not iron directly onto the knitting. You may need to readjust the pins once you steam the fabric. Let dry completely before you remove the pins.

Yarn Weight and Gauge

Yarn comes in several different weights from lace and fingerling to super bulky jumbo yarn. Each weight of yarn has a recommended needle size which will give you a specific gauge. Gauge refers to how many stitches it takes to create four inches of fabric across the rows, and how many rows it takes to create four inches of knit fabric.

It is a good practice to knit up a gauge swatch before you begin a pattern. Your tension may affect the gauge and you may need to go up or down a needle size to obtain the correct gauge. Knit up a swatch of material and count the stitches across a four-inch row. Now count the rows in four inches. This is the gauge.

In the following table you can see if you use a medium weight yarn with a size 7 to 9 needle you will have 16 to 20 stitches across a row of four inches. As the yarn weight increases or decreases, the gauge also increases or decreases.

This is why it is important to check the yarn and needle size for each pattern. If you use a yarn which is too light with small needles your project will be much smaller than you intended.

Yarn Weight Chart			
Weight	Description	Recommended Needle Size	Stitches in 4"
0 Lace	Fingerling, Size 10 Crochet Thread	000-1/1.5-2.25mm	33-40
1 Superfine	Sock, Fingerling	1-3/2.25-3.25mm	27-32
2 Fine	Sport, Baby	3-5/3.25-3.75mm	23-26
3 Light	DK, Light Worsted	5-7/3.75-4.5mm	21-24
4 Medium	Worsted, Afghan,	7-9/3.75-4.5mm	16-20

		Aran		
5	Bulky	Chunky, Craft, Rug	9-11/5.5-8mm	12-15
6	Super Bulky	Super Bulky, Roving	11-17/8-12.75mm	7-11
7	Jumbo	Jumbo, Roving	17/12.75mm and up	6 or less

How to Read a Yarn Label

When you go to purchase yarn, the information you need is all contained on the yarn label. The label will tell you the weight of the yarn, the gauge using the recommended needle size, and how to care for the finished project. It will also tell you what materials were used to create the yarn. Yarn manufacturers use a standardized set of laundry care symbols on their labels. You can find a complete list of these symbols at the Lion Brand site. I recommend printing the off and putting them near your washer and dryer for reference.

This yarn label is from a skein of Red Heart Super Saver Cherry Red yarn. As you can see, it is an acrylic yarn with a gauge of 17 stitches and 23 rows when using a size US 8 (5mm) needle. The weight class is 4, or medium. According to the laundry care symbols, this yarn can be machine washed and dried no hotter than 104F. The label also tells you the skein is center pull. Skeins pull from the center, while balls (which can also look like skiens) are pulled from the outside.

Knitting Needles

Knitting needles come in three main types: straight, circular, and double pointed. Straight needles are used for projects which are knitted back and forth in rows. Circular needles are used for knitting in the round, and to hold a large number of stitches in projects worked in rows. Double pointed needles allow you to knit small projects in the round such as hats and other project which would be too small to fit on a circular needle.

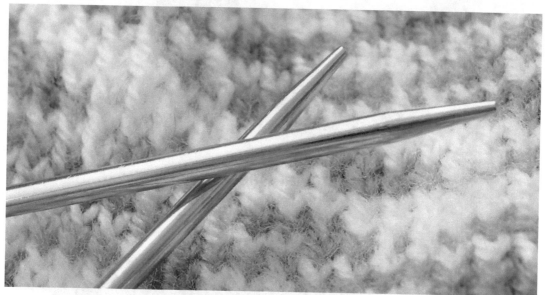

Straight Needles

Circular Needles

Double Pointed Needles

Other Equipment

Cable needles are curved needles used to hold stitches as you knit cables. Stitch holders look like huge safety pins and are used to hold a group of stitches while you knit. Row counters are handy to help you keep track of which row you are working on, and a flat or tapestry needle is also needed to weave in tails and sew pieces of knitting together. Markers are round circles which slip onto the needle to help you mark pattern repeats, the beginning of a round, and to guide you in a pattern. A good pair of scissors, or shears, is also an essential tool.

Chapter Two – Essential Knitting Stitches and Techniques

In this chapter we'll finally put some yarn on the needles and begin to knit. Remember if you're just starting out to take it slow. It will take a while to get used to handling the yarn and needles, so relax. You may have to rip out stitches, I still do. You may also drop some stitches, I still do that too. We'll learn how to pick up dropped stitches, and how to use a lifeline to help you if you have to rip out a section of your work. Concentrate on technique, not speed. Speed will come later with practice, for now enjoy yourself and relax!

Casting On

Before you actually knit any stitches you must first get the yarn onto the needles. This is known as casting on. In patterns you may see the abbreviation CO for cast on. In this section we'll learn some of my favorite and easy ways to cast on.

Backwards Loop Method

One of the easiest methods is the backwards loop method. Place a slip knot onto the needle. In your left hand hold the yarn with the yarn from the skein over your thumb and the tail over your index finger. With your right hand pull the yarn between your thumb and index finger down and insert the tip into the loop formed around your thumb. Release the yarn and wrap the yarn around the needle cast on the stitch. Repeat until you have the correct number of stitches cast on.

The advantage to the method is it is very quick and easy, but it makes a tight cast on row which can be hard to work with for beginners.

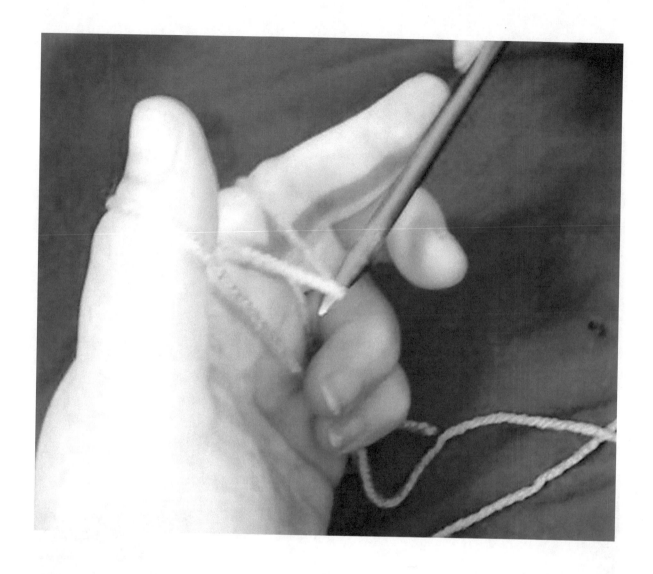

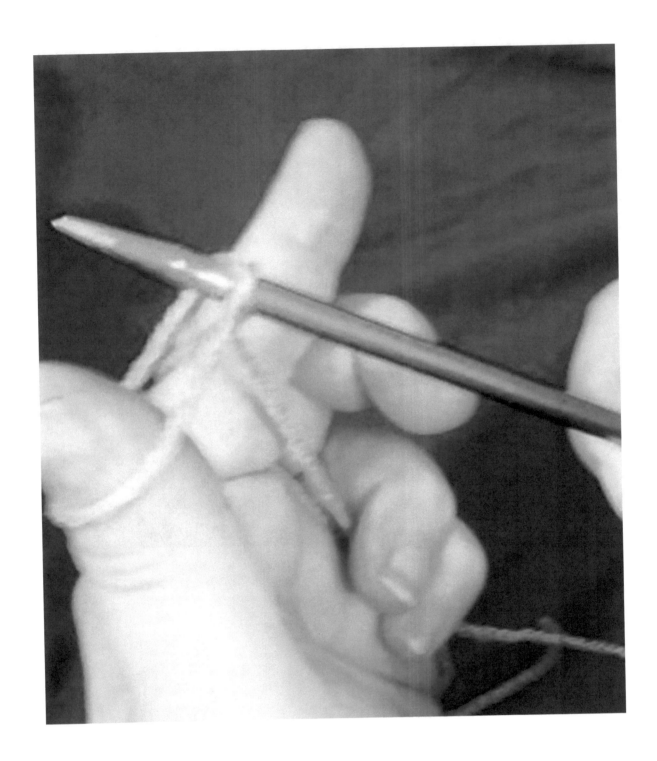

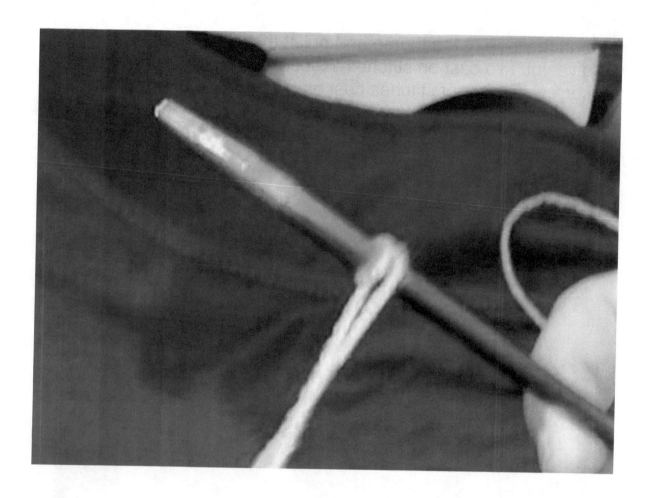

Long Tail Cast On

One of my favorite methods is the long tail cast on. It creates a nice even cast on row which is not too tight and is easy to work with. The disadvantage of this method is that you have to estimate how much yarn you need since you don't use the yarn coming off the skein. An easy way to estimate is to cast on 10 stitches and then mark how much yarn you used. Use this length to estimate how much yarn is needed for the cast on.

To begin hold the yarn like you did for the backward loop, but the yarn from the skein is held over the index finger, and the tail (which is what you'll be casting on) is held over your thumb. With your right hand draw the needle down and up through the loop on your thumb. Place the needle under the strand of yarn on the index finger and through the loop of the thumb and pull it through. The first cast on will give you two cast on stitches. Repeat the process until you have the correct number of stitches cast on.

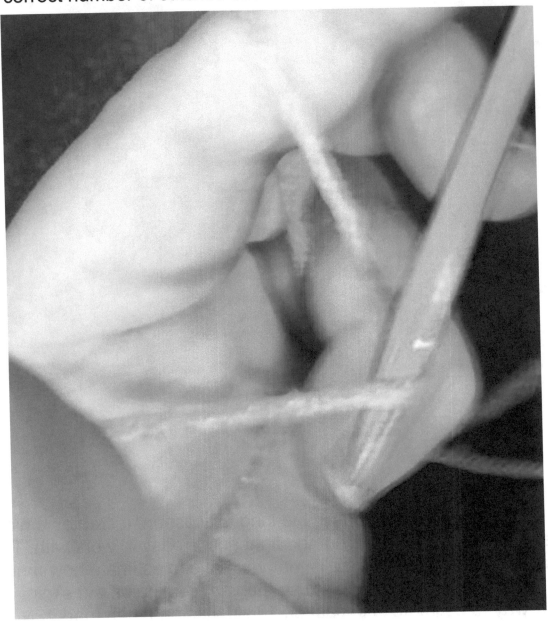

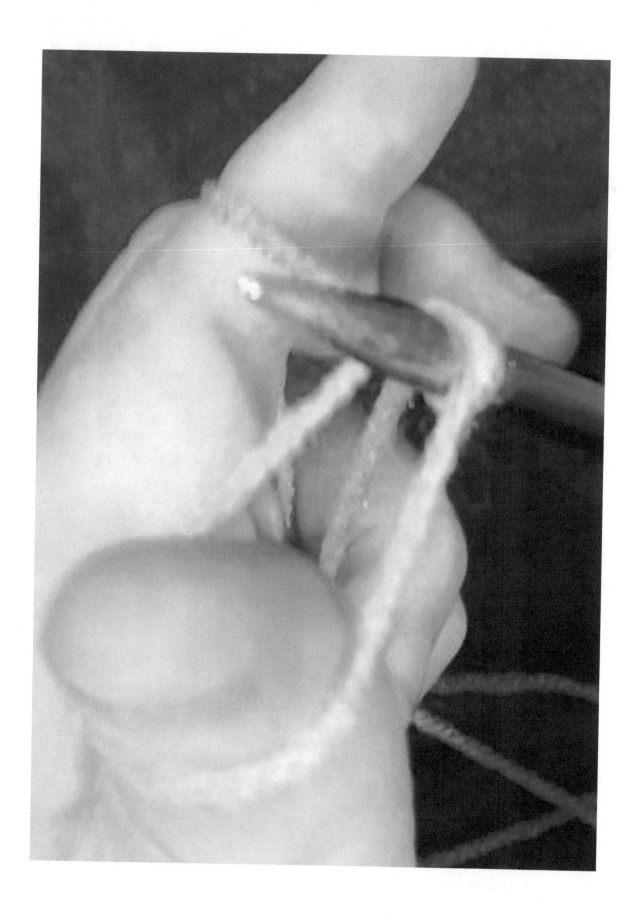

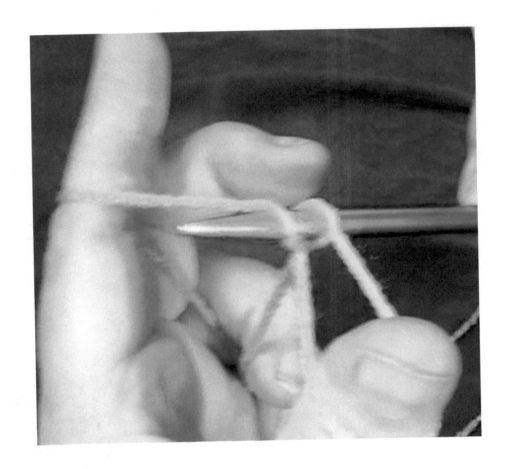

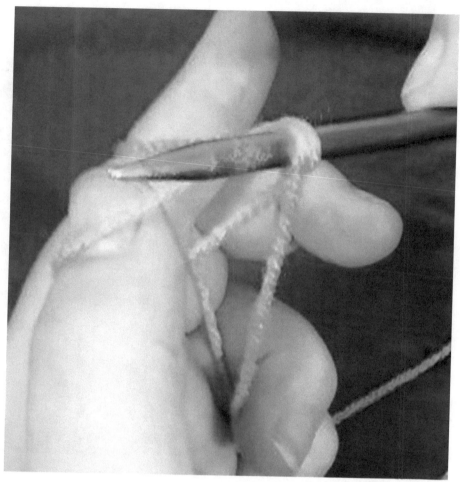

Knit On Cast On Method

Another cast on method I like to use is the knit on method. It produces a nice stretchy cast on row, and knits the first row for you. Begin by placing a slip knot on the left needle. Knit a stitch but don't slip it onto the right needle. Slip it back over onto the left needle instead. Knit the next stitch and slip the loop of that stitch back onto the left needle. Continue to knit stitches and slip them back onto the left needle until you have the correct number of cast on stitches.

Pull the loop of the knit stitch out a bit and then slip it back onto the left needle.

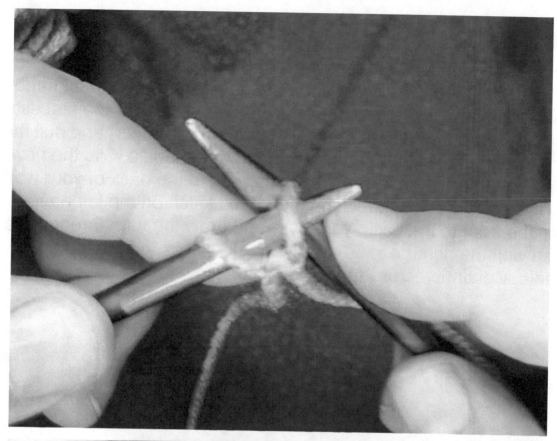

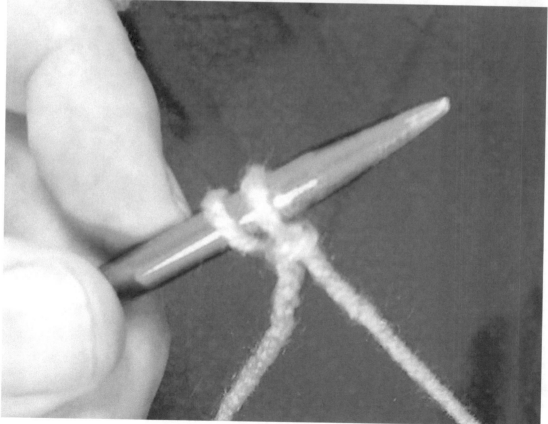

Knit Stitch

I'm right handed so the directions in this book are for right handed knitters. Hold the needle with the cast on stitches in your left hand. Insert the right needle from the front to the back under the first stitch. Wrap the yarn around the needle (known as yarn over) and pull the yarn through the stitch with the tip of the right needle. Slip the new stitch onto the right needle. Holing the yarn in the back of your work slip the tip of the right needle into the next stitch on the left needle from the front to the back, yarn over and draw the yarn through the stitch with the right needle and slip the new stitch onto the right needle. Continue across the row of stitches.

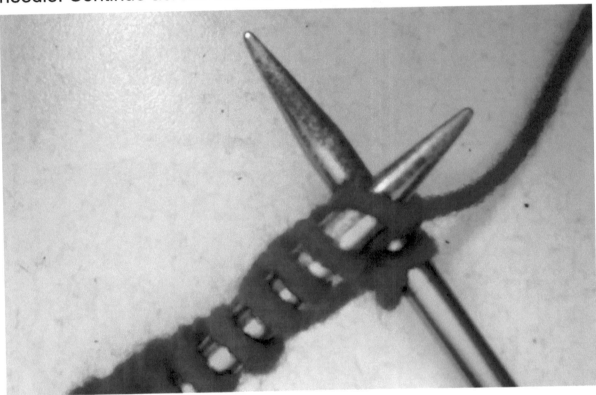

Wrap the yarn around the right needle.

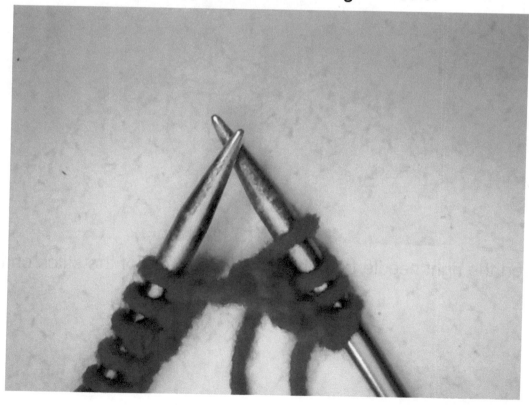

Pull the yarn through the stitch and slip it onto the right needle.

Purl Stitch

Hold the needle with the cast on stitches in your left hand. Insert the tip of the right needle into the first stitch from the back to the front. The tip of the right needle will be in front of the left one. Wrap the yarn around the right needle and draw it through the stitch and slip the new purl stitch onto the right needle. Hold the yarn in the front of your work and insert the needle from the back to the front into the next stitch on the left needle. Yarn

o   ver

and draw the yarn through the stitch and slip the new purl stitch onto the right needle. Continue across the row of stitches.

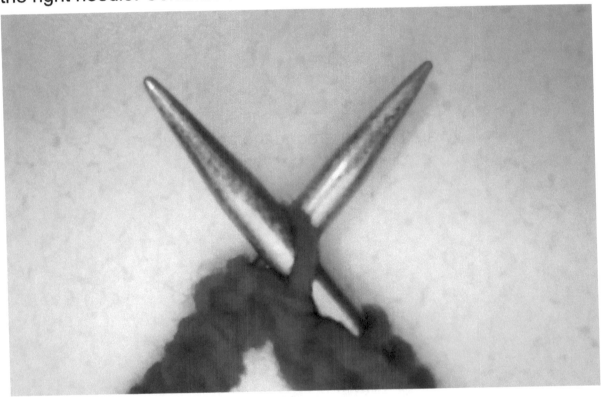

Insert the right needle from the back to the front of the stitch on the left needle.

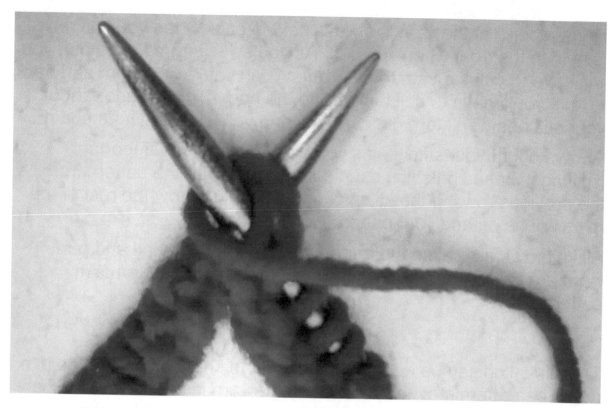

Wrap the yarn around the right needle.

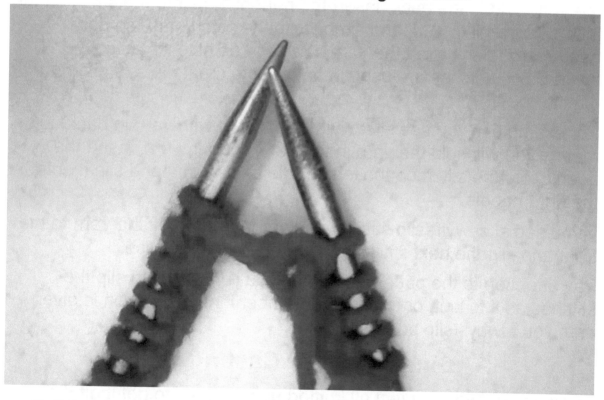

Pull the yarn through the stitch and slip it onto the right needle.

Remember that the yarn is always held in back when you knit, and it is held in the front when you purl. As you switch from knit to purl you will have to pull the yarn to the front. When you switch from purl back to knit, you'll have to pull the yarn to the back. This is important or your stitches won't turn out correctly and you'll be fighting the yarn.

Always count your stitches as you work. This is very important. Knitting is based on stitch counts and building up the pattern from the previous rows. If the stitch count is off in one row the rest of the rows will be off and your pattern won't be correct.

All knit rows are called the garter stitch. Alternating knit and purl rows are called stockinette stitch. You may see these terms in patterns.

Slip Stitches

The slip stitch can be done knitwise, as if to knit, or purlwise, as if to purl. The pattern may tell you to hold the yarn in the front or the back and which way to slip the stitch. If not, then assume it is knitwise with the yarn held in the back. Insert the right needle into the stitch on the left needle as if to purl, and simply slip the stitch onto the right needle. You don't wrap the yarn at all and no stitch is actually knitted. Slip stitches are used in patterns to create lots of different effects.

For example, if you see sl st wyib (slipt stitch with yarn in back) this means you will hold the yarn in the back of your work, insert the needle into the stitch on the left needle as if to purl and slip it onto the right needle.

If you see sl st wyif (slip stitch with yarn in front), pull the yarn to the front and slip the next stitch to the right needle purlwise.

Pay attention to the pattern, it will tell you if you should slip the stitches as if to knit, or to purl. Remember if no instruction is given, then you always slip purlwise.

Binding Off or Casting Off

Once you get your project all knitted up you have to get it off the needles. This is where you bind off, also known as casting off. You can bind of knitwise or purlwise depending on what your pattern calls for. If the pattern doesn't specify bind off knitwise. Knit the first two stitches. Now take the left needle and slip it under the first stitch and pull it over the second one and off the needle. Knit the next stitch and slip the first stitch over it. Continue to do that until you have only one stitch left on the needle. Remove it from the needle, cut the yarn (fasten off) and leave a long tail. Pull the tail through the last stitch and you're done!

Weaving in Tails Securely

When you fasten off the yarn leave at least six inches so you can weave it in securely. Thread a tapestry needle with the tail and weave it in and out of the stitches on the wrong side of the fabric for about an inch. Change direction and weave it in and out for another inch. Change direction once more and weave the tail in and out of the stitches. You may now cut the tail and be assured it won't come undone and start to unravel your project.

Changing Colors

Working with color is fun, and you shouldn't let it intimidate you. When you need to use another color simply pick it up and begin to work with it. Catch the old color under the yarn of the first stitch to secure it and prevent holes in your work. Knit a few stitches and then go back and snug up the yarn to secure the color change.

If you are changing colors at the end of a row and plan on using the color again very soon you can carry it up the side of your work. Let it hang on the side of the fabric and catch it under the yarn of the first stitch of a new row until you need it again up to about four rows. This secures it and you don't have as many tails to weave in.

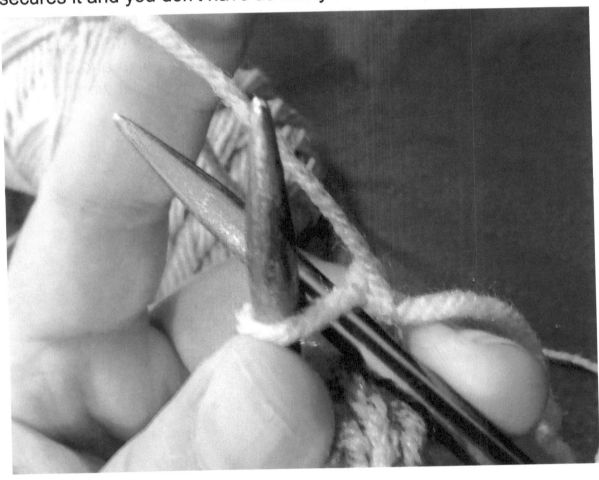

Picking Up a Dropped Stitch

We all drop stitches, it's just a fact of life when you knit. But you don't have to panic if you know how to fix it. You'll need a crochet hook and some patience. When you drop a stitch take the crochet hook and insert it through the loop of the stitch and grab the dropped stitch. Pull the yarn through the loop and place it back on the left needle. For a knit stitch you grab the yarn from the front and for a purl stitch grab the yarn from the back.

Life Lines

Life lines will save your sanity and your project. I use them a lot, even with simple patterns. With a life line if you mess up you don't have to rip out your entire project, you simply rip out rows to the lifeline and then pick up in the pattern and continue on. Thread a tapestry needle with a contrasting piece of yarn long enough to reach across the row. Thread the needle and yarn through the stitches on the needle and remove the tapestry needle. Now leave it. Mark the pattern where you inserted the life line. That way you can tell where you have ripped back to if you need to begin again. As you work move the lifeline up the pattern and make the pattern to keep track.

Designers use a standardized set of abbreviations in patterns. Here is a list of the most commonly used ones today.

Term	Abbreviation
Bind off	BO
Cast on	CO
Decrease	Dec
Increase	Inc
Knit	K
Knit 2 together	K2tog
Knitwise	kwise
Pattern Repeat	*, ( ), [ ]
Place marker	pm

Purl	P
Purl 2 together	P2tog
Purlwise	pwise
Repeat	Rep
Right side	RS
Skip	sk
Slip	sl
Wrong side	WS
Yarn over	Yo

Pattern Repeats

In a pattern you will see asterisks, parenthesis, and brackets with stitch instructions in them. These are pattern repeats. If asterisks are used begin at the first one and knit the stitches to the next one. Then go back to the first one and knit to the next one again. Repeat this as many times as the pattern calls for. For example *k, p3, k* mean you knit 1, purl 3, and knit 1. Then you go back and repeat this sequence as often as the pattern calls for.

Chapter Three – Ribbing

Ribbing us usually used at the cuffs of sleeves, on the bottoms of garments, and anywhere you want to add a bit of texture. Rib stitches are very stretchy so they make the perfect stitches for the openings on garments and at the brim of hats.

When you knit rib stitches you will line up the knit and purl stitches in each row or round. If you are knitting flat (in rows) you will knit and purl across the row, and then in the knit stitches you will purl, and into the purl stitches you will knit across the next row. This creates a ribbed pattern with the knit and purl stitches lined up on both sides of the fabric.

If you are knitting in the round, then you would just repeat the rib pattern around and around since you do not turn your work. The knit and purl stitches line up to create the ribbing pattern.

Knit 1, Purl 1 Ribbing

Cast on an even number of stitches and knit 1, purl 1 across the row. Turn your work. You should have ended with a purl stitch so the first stitch of the new row should be a knit stitch. The knit and purl stiches should line up on both sides of the fabric. If you are knitting in the round, knit 1, purl 1 around each row since you don't turn your work.

Knit 2, Purl 2 Ribbing

Cast on sets of 4. This means the number of stitches cast on must be divisible by the number 4. Knit 2, purl 2 across the row. Turn your work. Now if you have ended with knit stitches, the first 2 stitches will be purl. If you have ended with purl stitches, the first 2 stitches are knit. This lines up the ribbing pattern in sets of 2.

If you are knitting in the round, just repeat knit 2, purl 2 around the rounds making sure you keep on track and line up the knit and purl stitches.

Notice how the stitches line up to create ribbing.

Knit 2, Purl 3 Ribbing

Begin by casting on sets of 6. Knit 3, purl3 across the row and turn your work. Now if you have ended with knit stitches, the first 3 stitches will be purl. If you have ended with purl stitches, the first 3 stitches are knit. This lines up the ribbing pattern in sets of 3. If you are knitting in the round, just repeat knit 2, purl 2 around the rounds making sure you keep on track and line up the knit and purl stitches.

Staggered Ribbing

You can also create a pretty ribbing pattern by staggering your stitches. In this example I knit 1, purl 1, knit 1 across the row. The actual knitting is k1, p1 *k2, p1* to the last stitch which is a knit stitch. The stitches between the two asterisks are repeated to the last stitch. This an example of a pattern repeat.

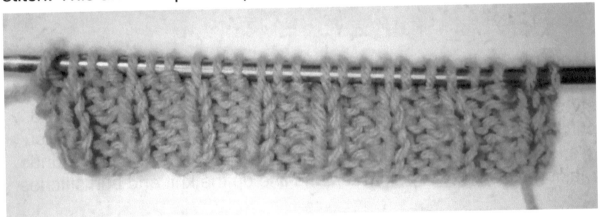

Right Side

Wrong Side

Experiment with different ribbing patterns. You can have ribbing as small as 1 by 1, or as wide as you like. Just remember if you're working in rows your knit stitches become purl stitches in the next row. This is because when you turn your work you will need to line up the stitches to retain the rib pattern. If you're working in the round then you just continue the ribbing pattern around the rounds.

Chapter Four – Texture with Knit and Purl Stitches

In this chapter we'll explore some fun and creative ways to use simple knit and purl stitches to create texture and patterns in your projects. One of the great things about using knit and purl stitches is most projects are double sided. The right side will have a different texture then the wrong side, but there will be texture and patterns on both sides of the fabric.

Stockinette Stitch

The stockinette stitch is knitted in a two row pattern. The first row is knitted and the second row is purled. The right side of the fabric is smooth with V's of stitches lined up in rows. The wrong side of the fabric is bumpy and has what are known as purl bumps. When knitting in rows you will knit one row and purl the next. If you are knitting in the round then you would only have to knit each row since you don't turn your work.

Right Side

Wrong Side

Garter Stitch

The garter stitch is very easy. You knit each row. This creates a lovely texture and the garter stitch does not roll up like the stockinette stitch. If you are knitting in the round, then you would need to purl each row to achieve the same look. The right and wrong side look exactly alike since you are knitting all rows.

By combing stockinette and garter stitches you can create patterns and texture in you knit projects. You can also use garter and stockinette stitches to create a frame for your projects.

In this example you can see how rows of garter stitches form the top and bottom "frame" for this dishcloth. The knit stitches on the sides keep the dishcloth from rolling up and also create a frame for the basket weave stitches.

You can also see how combining knit and purl stitches and alternating them creates a basket weave effect. (I'll include the pattern for this dishcloth at the end of this book.)

By alternating stockinette and garter rows you can also frame a feature of a pattern. In this bag pattern the eyelet stitches are framed by rows of garter stitches which make them pop. Without the garter rows, the eyelet pattern wouldn't be as striking.

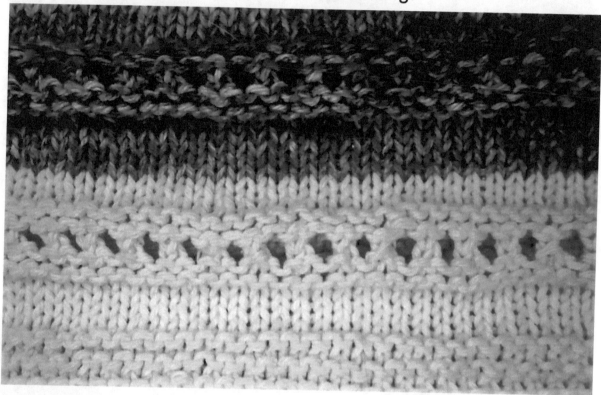

Using Knit and Purl Stitches to Create Patterns

In the basket weave dishcloth, you can see how using knit and purl stitches create a pretty pattern. You can also use knit and purl stitches to create patterns and pictures in your knitting.

In the following examples you can see how using knit and purl stitches create a pretty heart design. You can use this technique to create any type of pattern or picture you want in your projects. Also notice the garter rows and knit stitches which form a frame and keep the square from rolling up on itself.

Seed Stitch

The seed stitch creates a bumpy fabric which is great for dishcloths and washcloths. It is also a nice addition of texture to a project. Unlike ribbing you will be working knit stitches into knit stitches and purl stitches into the purl stitches on the next row. This staggers the purl bumps and creates a pretty texture.

Cast on an even number of stitches. Knit 1, purl 1 across the row. Turn your work. Purl 1, knit 1 across the next row. Alternate the rows until you have the desired length.

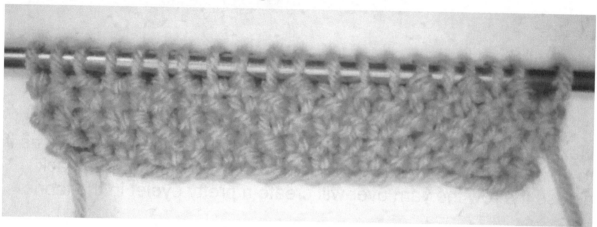

Eyelet Stitch

The eyelet stitch is a combination of knit and yarn overs. A yarn over is exactly what it sounds like, you place the yarn over the needle before you knit two stitches together.

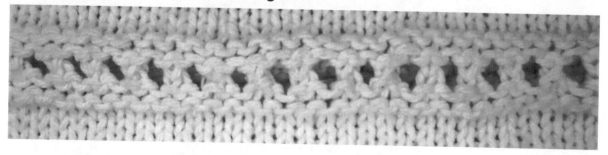

First place the yarn over the right needle.

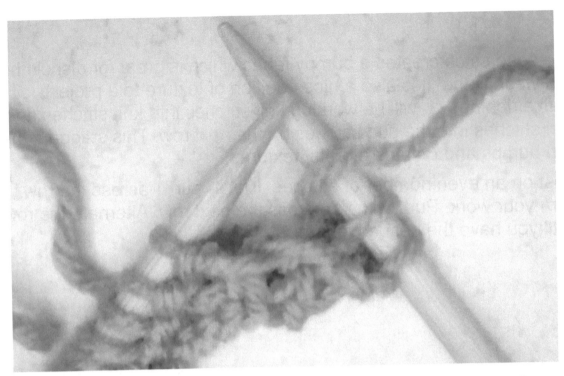

Next insert the right needle under two stitches on the left needle as if to nit. Knit both stitches together. Now when you knit or purl back across the row the yarn over will create a pretty eyelet in the fabric.

Drop Stitch

The drop stitch is a fun way to add a lot of texture and interest to your projects. It also uses yarn overs and knit stitches. First yarn over once or twice depending on the look you want. Knit the next stitch. Continue to yarn over and knit across the row. It works best if you knit the first two and the last two stitches of the drop stitch row.

When you come back across the row, knit or purl the knit stitches and let the yarn overs fall of the needle. It may seem strange to drop stitches on purpose, but this is what creates the pattern.

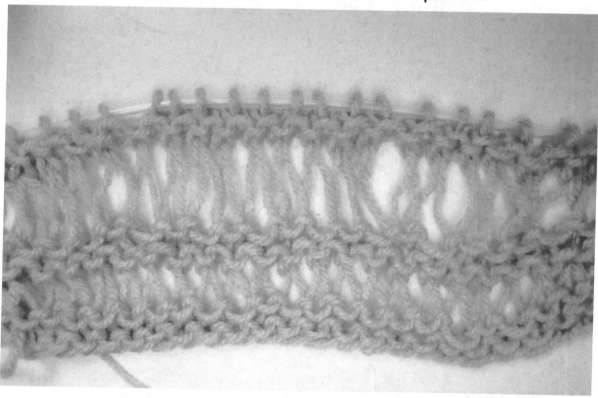

The first set of drop stitches is a single yarn over. The top set of drop stitches were created with two yarn overs. You can see how the double yarn over creates a much looser texture.

Chapter Five – Fun Beginner Patterns

Now that we've learned the basics of knitting and how you can use knit and purl stitches to create texture in knitting, let's practice with some simply beginner patterns. Refer to the abbreviation table in Chapter Two for the patterns in this chapter.

Basket Weave Dishcloth

You will need a skein each of cotton yarn in two colors. I used Premier Home yarn in Violet Splash (Color A) and Sahara Splash (Color B)

The pattern is knitted in sets of 5 plus 6. So you can make the washcloth larger or smaller as long as you cast on sets of 5 and then 6 more for the edging stitches.

With Color A CO 31

Rows 1-3: k

Row 4: k3 *p5, k5* rep ending with p5, k3

Row 5: k3 *k5, p5* rep ending with k5, k3

Row 6: Repeat Row 4

Row 7: Repeat Row 5

Row 8: Repeat Row 4

Row 9: k3 * p5, k5* rep ending with p5, k3

Row 10: k3 *k5, p5* rep ending with k5, k3

Row 11: Repeat Row 9

Row 12: Repeat Row 10

Row 13: Repeat Row 9

With Color B

Rows 14-23: Repeat Rows 4-13

With Color A

Rows 24-32: Repeat Rows 4-13

Rows 33-35: k, BO and weave in tails.

Drop Stitch Scarf

Cowl measures about 9 inches wide and around 58-60 inches long.

You will need size 15 (10mm) knitting needles and 1 skein of Premier Home yarn in Grape Splash. You will also need a tapestry needle. (You can use any yarn you have on hand. If you use a thicker yarn the cowl will be shorter, but still very pretty.)

Gauge is not important for this project.

Cast on 30

Row 1 & 2: k

Row 3: k1 *yo twice, k1* rep to last st, k1

Row 3-5: k

Row: 6: k1, *yo, k1* rep to last st, k1

Rows 12-16: k

Rows 13-30: Repeat Rows 6-12 twice

Row 31: k1 *yo twice, k1* rep to last st, k1

Rows 32-38: k

Row 39: k1, *yo, k1* rep to last st, k1

Rows 40-45: k

Rows 46-57: Repeat Rows 39-45 twice

Row 58: k1 *yo twice, k1* rep to last st, k1

Rows 59-64: k

Row 65: k1, *yo, k1* rep to last st, k1

Rows 66-70: k

Rows 71-82: Repeat Rows 65-70 twice

Row 83: *yo twice, k1* rep to last st, k1

Rows 84-89: k

Row 90: k1, *yo, k1* rep to last st, k1

Rows 91-96: k

Rows 97-103: Repeat Rows 90-96

0Row 104: k1, *yo, k1* rep to last st, k1

Rows 105-107: k, cast off knitwise after Row 107, weave in tails and block lightly with your hands.

Add fringe on the ends if you'd like. You could also sew the end together to make a cute infinity scarf.

Seed Stitch Square

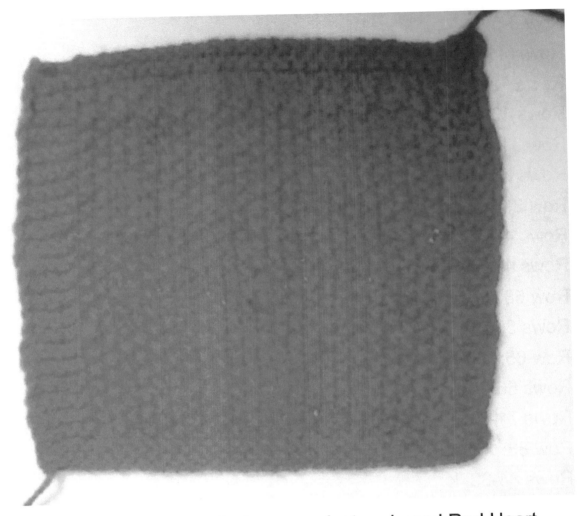

I knitted this up to be part of a larger project and used Red Heart Super Saver in Hot Pink, but you can use cotton yarn and make this pattern into a dishcloth or wash cloth.

CO 30

Rows 1-3: k

Row 4: k4 *k1, p1* k4

Row 5-34: Repeat Row 4

Rows 35-37: k

BO and weave in tails

Eyelet Cowl

I really like to knit up cowls. They work up quickly and make great gifts. I used knit, purl, yarn over and knit 2 together stitches to create a highly textured pattern which looks much more complicated than it really is.

You will need a skein of acrylic or any medium weight yarn. I used Red Heart Super Saver in Shocking Pink. You will also need a 24 inch size 8 circular needle and a tapestry needle.

Cast on 150

Rnds 1 & 2: k

Rnd 3: p

Rnd 4: k

Rnd 5: p

Rnd 6: *yo, k2tog, k1* rep around

Rnd 7: *k1, yo, k2tog* rep around

Rnds 8-14: k

Rnd 15-19: Rep Rnds 3-7

Rnd 20: p

Rnd 21: k

Rnd 22: p

Rnds 23 & 24: k

BO and weave in tails.

Thank you for purchasing this book on using knit and purl stitches to create texture in your knitting projects. Feel free to sell anything you make from the patterns in this book, but please share the link to the book if you want to share a pattern.

I hope you enjoy learning how to knit and experimenting with texture in your projects. Until next time take care!